THE ROUGH GUIDE TO

World Cup

2002 Japan • Korea

Edited by
Dan Goldstein

G000138176

ROUGH
GUIDES

Editor, design and layout: Dan Goldstein
Commissioning editor: Jonathan Buckley
Production: Andy Turner, Susanne Hillen
Photography: Empics, Nottingham, England
Special thanks to: Ben Cole, Tim Graham, Hubi Gross, Nick Moody,
    Jan Purath, Phillip Smith

....

This first edition published April 2002 by **Rough Guides Ltd**, 62–70 Shorts
    Gardens, London WC2H 9AH.
Distributed by the Penguin Group
Penguin Books Ltd, 80 Strand, London WC2R 0RL
Penguin Putnam Inc., 345 Hudson Street, NY 10014, USA
Penguin Books Australia Ltd, 487 Maroondah Highway, PO Box 257, Ringwood,
    Victoria 3134, Australia
Penguin Books Canada Ltd, 10 Alcorn Avenue, Toronto, Ontario, Canada M4V 1E4
Penguin Books (NZ) Ltd, 182–190 Wairau Road, Auckland 10, New Zealand

Printed in Italy by LegoPrint S.p.A

96pp
A catalogue record for this book is available from the British Library
ISBN 1-84353-107-0

....

CONTENTS

The teams

PREVIOUS TOURNAMENTS

Uruguay 1930 No. of teams entered 13
Final – Montevideo, 30 July
Uruguay 4 (Dorado 12, Cea 58, Iriarte 68, Castro 89)
Argentina 2 (Pecuelle 20, Stábile 38)

Italy 1934 No. of teams entered 16; in qualifying 29
Final – Rome, 10 June
Italy 2 (Orsi 81, Schiavio 95)
Czechoslovakia 1 (Puc 71) (*after extra time*)

France 1938 No. of teams entered 15; in qualifying 27
Final – Paris, 19 June
Italy 4 (Colaussi 6, 35, Piola 16, 82)
Hungary 2 (Titkos 8, Sárosi 70)

Brazil 1950 No. of teams entered 13; in qualifying 25
Deciding match – Rio de Janeiro, 16 July
Uruguay 2 (Schiaffino 66, Ghiggia 79)
Brazil 1 (Friaça 47)

Switzerland 1954 No. of teams entered 16; in qualifying 36
Final – Berne, 4 July
West Germany 3 (Morlock 11, Rahn 18, 84)
Hungary 2 (Puskás 6, Czibor 9)

Sweden 1958 No. of teams entered 16; in qualifying 48
Final – Stockholm, 29 June
Brazil 5 (Vavá 9, 32, Pelé 55, 90, Zagallo 68)
Sweden 2 (Liedholm 4, Simonsson 80)

Chile 1962 No. of teams entered 16; in qualifying 51
Final – Santiago, 17 June
Brazil 3 (Amarildo 17, Zito 69, Vavá 78)
Czechoslovakia 1 (Masopust 16)

England 1966 No. of teams entered 16; in qualifying 53
Final – London, 30 July
England 4 (Hurst 18, 101, 120, Peters 78)
West Germany 2 (Haller 12, Weber 90) (*after extra time*)

Mexico 1970 No. of teams entered 16; in qualifying 70
Final – Mexico City, 21 June
Brazil 4 (Pelé 18, Gérson 66, Jairzinho 71, Carlos Alberto 87)
Italy 1 (Boninsegna 37)

West Germany 1974 No. of teams entered 16; in qualifying 92
Final – Munich, 7 July
West Germany 2 (Breitner 25 pen, Müller 43)
Holland 1 (Neeskens 2 pen)

Argentina 1978 No. of teams entered 16; in qualifying 96
Final – Buenos Aires, 25 June
Argentina 3 (Kempes 38, 105, Bertoni 115)
Holland 1 (Nanninga 82) (*after extra time*)

Spain 1982 No. of teams entered 24; in qualifying 105
Final – Madrid, 11 July
Italy 3 (Rossi 57, Tardelli 69, Altobelli 81)
West Germany 1 (Breitner 83)

Mexico 1986 No. of teams entered 24; in qualifying 113
Final – Mexico City, 29 June
Argentina 3 (Brown 23, Valdano 56, Burruchaga 85)
West Germany 2 (Rummenigge 74, Völler 82)

Italy 1990 No. of teams entered 24; in qualifying 105
Final – Rome, 8 July
West Germany 1 (Brehme 85 pen)
Argentina 0

USA 1994 No. of teams entered 24; in qualifying 133
Final – Los Angeles, 17 July
Brazil 0
Italy 0 (*after extra time; Brazil won 3–2 on pens*)

France 1998 No. of teams entered 32; in qualifying 170
Final – Paris, 12 July
France 3 (Zidane 27, 45, Petit 90)
Brazil 0

FIXTURE SCHEDULE

Group A

31–5–02	Seoul	France	–	Senegal
1–6–02	Ulsan	Uruguay	–	Denmark
6–6–02	Busan	France	–	Uruguay
6–6–02	Daegu	Denmark	–	Senegal
11–6–02	Suwon	Senegal	–	Uruguay
11–6–02	Incheon	Denmark	–	France

Group B

2–6–02	Busan	Paraguay	–	South Africa
2–6–02	Gwangju	Spain	–	Slovenia
7–6–02	Jeonju	Spain	–	Paraguay
8–6–02	Deagu	South Africa	–	Slovenia
12–6–02	Daejeon	South Africa	–	Spain
12–6–02	Seogwipo	Slovenia	–	Paraguay

Group C

3–6–02	Ulsan	Brazil	–	Turkey
4–6–02	Gwangju	China	–	Costa Rica
8–6–02	Seogwipo	Brazil	–	China
9–6–02	Incheon	Costa Rica	–	Turkey
13–6–02	Suwon	Costa Rica	–	Brazil
13–6–02	Seoul	Turkey	–	China

Group D

4–6–02	Busan	South Korea	–	Poland
5–6–02	Suwon	USA	–	Portugal
10–6–02	Daegu	South Korea	–	USA
10–6–02	Jeonju	Portugal	–	Poland
14–6–02	Incheon	Portugal	–	South Korea
14–6–02	Daejeon	Poland	–	USA

Group E

1–6–02	Niigata	Ireland	–	Cameroon
1–6–02	Sapporo	Germany	–	Saudi Arabia
5– 6–02	Ibaraki	Germany	–	Ireland
6–6–02	Saitama	Cameroon	–	Saudi Arabia
11–6–02	Shizuoka	Cameroon	–	Germany
11–6–02	Yokohama	Saudi Arabia	–	Ireland

Group F

2–6–02	Saitama	England	–	Sweden
2–6–02	Ibaraki	Argentina	–	Nigeria
7–6–02	Kobe	Sweden	–	Nigeria
7–6–02	Sapporo	Argentina	–	England
12–6–02	Miyagi	Sweden	–	Argentina
12–6–02	Osaka	Nigeria	–	England

Group G

3–6–02	Niigata	Croatia	–	Mexico
3–6–02	Sapporo	Italy	–	Ecuador
8–6–02	Ibaraki	Italy	–	Croatia
9–6–02	Miyagi	Mexico	–	Ecuador
13–6–02	Oita	Mexico	–	Italy
13–6–02	Yokohama	Ecuador	–	Croatia

Group H

4–6–02	Saitama	Japan	–	Belgium
5–6–02	Kobe	Russia	–	Tunisia
9–6–02	Yokohama	Japan	–	Russia
10–6–02	Oita	Tunisia	–	Belgium
14–6–02	Osaka	Tunisia	–	Japan
14–6–02	Shizuoka	Belgium	–	Russia

Second round

15–6–02	Seogwipo	winners E	–	runners-up B
15–6–02	Niigata	winners A	–	runners-up F
16–6–02	Oita	winners F	–	runners-up A
16–6–02	Suwon	winners B	–	runners-up E
17–6–02	Jeonju	winners G	–	runners-up D
17–6–02	Kobe	winners C	–	runners-up H
18–6–02	Miyagi	winners H	–	runners-up C
18–6–02	Daejeon	winners D	–	runners-up G

Quarter-finals

21–6–02	Shizuoka	winners Niigata	–	winners Kobe
21–6–02	Ulsan	winners Seogwipo	–	winners Jeonju
22–6–02	Gwangju	winners Suwon	–	winners Daejeon
22–6–02	Osaka	winners Oita	–	winners Miyagi

Semi–finals

25–6–02	Seoul	winners Ulsan	–	winners Gwangju
26–6–02	Saitama	winners Shizuoka	–	winners Osaka

Third-place play-off

| 29–6–02 | Daegu | losers Seoul | – | losers Saitama |

Final

| 30–6–02 | Yokohama | winners Seoul | – | winners Saitama |

Referees (by confederation)

AFC
Ali Bujsaim (UAE)
Toru Kamikawa (Japan)
Kim Young Joo (South Korea)
Lu Jun (China)
Saad Kamel Mane (Kuwait)

CAF
Coffi Codiha (Benin)
Mourad Daami (Tunisia)
Ndoye Falla (Senegal)
Gamal Ghandour (Egypt)
Mohammed Guezzaz (Morocco)

CONCACAF
Carlos Batres (Guatemala)
Brian Hall (USA)
William Mattus Vega (Costa Rica)
Peter Prendergast (Jamaica)
Felipe Ramos Rizo (Mexico)

OFC
Mark Shield (Australia)

CONMEBOL
Ubaldo Aquino (Paraguay)
Jorge Larrionda (Uruguay)
Byron Moreno (Ecuador)
Oscar Julian Ruiz (Colombia)
Angel Sanchez (Argentina)
Carlos Eugenio Simon (Brazil)

UEFA
Pierluigi Collina (Italy)
Hugh Dallas (Scotland)
Anders Frisk (Sweden)
Terje Hauge (Norway)
António Lopez Nieto (Spain)
Lubos Michel (Slovakia)
Markus Merk (Germany)
Urs Meier (Switzerland)
Vítor Melo Pereira (Portugal)
Kim Milton Nielsen (Denmark)
Graham Poll (England)
Kyros Vassaras (Greece)
Gilles Veissiere (France)
Jan Wegereef (Holland)

THE TEAMS: INTRODUCTION

As in France last time around, these World Cup finals will bring 32 of the globe's most talented national football teams together in one place (or, to be more accurate, two places). They are divided into eight groups of four, who will all play each other once only, earning three points for a win and one for a draw. When all the teams have played each other, the group phase is over and the top two nations in each group table will proceed to the knockout phase – second round, quarter-finals, semi-finals and final.

Uniquely in World Cup history, the 2002 is being co-hosted by Japan and South Korea – a **compromise solution** forced on FIFA once it had decided that Asia should take its place among the roster of World Cup hosts, only to realise that neither country was likely to have sufficient resources to accommodate all the matches on its own.

The groups have been organised in such a way that each one will take place in either Japan or Korea, and not be divided between the two. All the same, with so many host venues (10 in each country), the amount of travelling involved will be substantial, with many teams – not to mention their supporters – being obliged to take internal flights at various points in the proceedings.

With the Japanese and Koreans **both qualifying automatically**, and France also having booked their ticket by winning the World Cup in 1998, there were 29 places up for grabs when the qualifying tournament kicked-off in the spring of 2000. These were gradually taken until Uruguay became the last nation to qualify by beating Australia in November 2001.

Of those that will be in Japan and Korea, the **French remain the favourites** in the eyes of many, provided there is still enough desire in a team which has won every competition it has entered since '98. Argentina probably run them a close second, their squad superior on paper but their temperament still suspect. Brazil and Germany, powerhouses of the world game but currently in the process of rebuilding, have been written off by many pundits, but Italy, runners-up to France in the last European Championship, are taking some smart money as dark horses.

Also worth watching are the **perennial also-rans** Spain and Portugal, whose teams are at the peak of their powers; a rejuvenated Russia; Cameroon, recently crowned champions of Africa for the second time in a row; and Poland, who make a welcome return to the World Cup after a 26-year absence. Finally, neither England nor Ireland go into the competition expecting to win it. But then, stranger things have happened.

DENMARK

The Danes have a simple and perhaps intractable problem – most of their talent is in the dugout, rather than on the pitch. The coaching combination of Morten Olsen and Michael Laudrup in theory offers the team a winning combination of discipline and flair. In reality, the limitations of a hard-working, motivated but ultimately uninspiring group of players may lead to Denmark leaving the World Cup party early, echoing the nation's drab showing at Euro 2000.

THE PEDIGREE

While Denmark's best performance at a major international tournament was their Cinderella-style triumph at Euro '92, the World Cup has also seen the team upset the form-book. Most famously, in **Mexico** in 1986 a fearless team led by current coach Olsen and inspired by his assistant Laudrup romped to three successive group-stage wins over Scotland, Uruguay and West Germany – before inexplicably losing the plot in a 5–1 second-round defeat by Spain.

Four years ago in **France**, Laudrup (sole survivor of the *Danish Dynamite* class of '86) returned for a last hurrah, his improvisational attacking balanced by the seemingly immovable object of goalkeeper Peter Schmeichel at the other end of the park. After qualifying from the group stages unconvincingly, the Danes crushed Nigeria 4–1 before giving Brazil the fright of their lives in the quarter-finals.

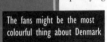

The fans might be the most colourful thing about Denmark

THE ROAD TO JAPAN/KOREA

Unbeaten in a group where their closest rivals (Bulgaria and the Czech Republic) conspired to drop points in unlikely places, the Danes qualified for the finals convincingly enough. As usual, they were at their most impressive in Copenhagen, where boisterous, colourful support and a tight pitch fazed visitors.

Goalkeeper **Thomas Sorensen** conceded just six goals in ten games, while the Italian-based midfield pairing of **Thomas Helveg** and **Martin Jorgensen** ensured that while the Danes rarely monopolised possession as efficiently as Europe's best, they usually made the most of what they had. When your game is based on quick counter-attacking, it helps to have pace upfront, and while **Ebbe Sand** (see below) scored the biggest share of Denmark's 22 goals in qualifying, strike partner John Dahl Tomasson got two of the most important – a morale-reviving equaliser in the team's opener in Iceland, followed by the winner at home to the Czechs.

THE KEY PLAYER The anthithesis of Scandinavia's clichéd lumbering frontman, **Ebbe Sand** combines versatility with reliability. His brisk acceleration catches opposing defences off-guard during Denmark's trademark breakaway moves, while a full repertoire of flicks and lay-offs bring supporting team-mates expertly into play.

Unlike many strikers of his generation, Sand seems capable of maintaining his form for club and country simultaneously. His 22 goals took Schalke to within a whisker of the German *Bundesliga* title in 2000/01, while his World Cup qualifying tally of nine included a hat-trick in Malta.

He will do well, though, to match the drama of his performance at France '98, when he scored 24 seconds into his international debut after coming on as a substitute against Nigeria.

THE EMERGING TALENT Seemingly anonymous amid a wave of Scandinavian imports to have come to the English Premiership with bargain price-tags around their necks, Charlton's **Claus Jensen** is beginning to look a class apart.

Jensen signed from Bolton for £4million in the July 2000, three months after making his full international debut for Denmark. His unhurried, almost languid style helps to conceal a formidable 'engine', and while defensive duties come less naturally, the English game has made Jensen both more aggressive and more conscientious.

THE DUGOUT Denmark's legendary former captain **Morten Olsen** took charge of his country after Euro 2000. He has been assisted from the beginning by **Michael Laudrup**, a former team-mate who concentrates on one-to-one coaching while Olsen works on strategy. While Laudrup is set to leave his post after the World Cup – to be replaced by Keld Bordinggaard – Olsen has signed a new contract which will keep him head coach for at least a further two years.

FRANCE

The only team ever to win the European Championship with the World Cup already in their trophy cabinet, France remain top of many pundits' lists to retain the latter prize in 2002. It's not hard to see why. The defensive solidity built by coach Aimé Jacquet on home soil in 1998 was given a dose of irrepressible attacking flair by his successor Roger Lemerre at Euro 2000. If the two elements can be combined successfully in Japan and Korea, then the French will be harder to defeat than ever.

THE PEDIGREE

The World Cup and the European Championship were both French inventions, yet it took a long time for France's footballers to make as big a mark on the game as the country's administrators. After a series of false dawns, a side led by the brilliant Michel Platini won the European crown on home soil in 1984. At the **Mexico** World Cup two years later, the same team played some of the tournament's most majestic football before losing to West Germany in the semi-finals – just as they had done in **Spain** four years earlier.

With the domestic game mired in bribery scandals and other financial disasters for much of the 1990s, the national team failed to qualify for the finals at all in that decade – until host-nation status did the trick automatically in 1998. The rest is (recent) history: Blanc's last-ditch winner against Paraguay; Barthez out-psyching the Italians in a quarter-final shoot-out; Thuram leading a memorable comeback against Croatia in the semis; Zidane stealing in unmarked to build an impregnable lead in the final against a much-hyped Brazil.

THE ROAD TO JAPAN/KOREA

After a FIFA rule change which went almost unnoticed when it was announced last year, France are the last team to qualify for the World Cup finals automatically as holders. Not that they have been slumbering in the intervening period. While the rest of the planet was engaged in qualifying games, the French won the (admittedly fairly meaningless) Confederations Cup in Japan last year. A year before that, there was the small matter of being crowned champions of Europe.

THE KEY PLAYER

As unobtrusive as he is elegant, **Zinedine Zidane** is still the creative force against which all French (and most

European) midfielders are measured. Arguably an even more influential presence at Euro 2000 than he had been at the World Cup two years earlier, 'Zizou' comes into this tournament at the peak of his powers.

When Real Madrid paid Juventus a world-record fee of £47million for Zidane in the summer of 2001, they were buying a player whose talents had made him World Footballer of the Year twice in the preceding three seasons. Yet for the coaches who pick him to work his magic 'in the hole' between midfield and attack, Zidane's great appeal is that he is as hard-working now as he was in 1984, when he watched Platini's European Champions as a ball-boy on the edge of the Marseilles Vélodrome pitch.

THE EMERGING TALENT
No more than a bit-part player in France's Euro 2000 triumph, **Robert Pires** looks set to play a much more pivotal role in the team's defence of their World Cup crown. With the side ageing and slowing in some departments, Pires' pace and energy should give the French an alternative creative outlet – particularly handy if Zinedine Zidane is tightly marked.

Though used as a midfielder by both his country and his club, Arsenal, Pires can also play in more advanced positions, and his understanding with his club-mate Thierry Henry can only widen the scope of his influence for *Les Bleus*.

Robert Pires has been tipped for glory by Arsène Wenger

THE DUGOUT
With Jacquet moving 'upstairs' following France '98, **Roger Lemerre** took over as national-team coach, and immediately set about putting his own imprint on the squad. His move to a more attacking game was criticised in some quarters, but he is instinctively trusted by the players, many of whom owe their progress to the youth programme Lemerre put in place alongside Gérard Houllier in the mid-1990s.

SENEGAL

The running joke is that when Senegal and France take the field for the World Cup's opening game in Seoul on 31 May, the Senegalese side will contain more French players than the holders'. Of the 22-man squad which earned Senegal runners-up spot at the 2002 African Nations Cup, 19 were based with French clubs, many having been born in France of Senegalese descent. (On the other hand, France's Patrick Vieira was born in Senegal.) With such a rich body of top-level playing talent at its disposal, the only wonder is that it has taken so long for this west African nation to reach the most elevated footballing stage.

THE PEDIGREE

Prior to 2001, Senegal had never come close to qualifying for the World Cup finals. They have been regular if undistinguished participants in the African Nations Cup, where their best finish was a semi-final place under Claude Le Roy in 1990.

THE ROAD TO JAPAN/KOREA

After struggling to overcome tiny Benin in the first qualifying round, Senegal were thrown into the toughest of Africa's five group-stage sections alongside Morocco, Egypt and Algeria – previous qualifiers all. But while some of the more illustrious names struggled to find their form, the 'Dakar Lions' began to exhibit the tough backbone that would allow them to exploit their rivals' unease.

Highly rated young 'keeper **Tony Mario Sylva** conceded just one goal in Senegal's first five games, the defence in front of him efficiently marshalled by the quietly impressive **Ferdinand Coly**. A 1–0 loss in Egypt was Senegal's first of the series – and it would be their last.

Favourites Morocco remained group leaders but, crucially, they lost their last game – in Dakar. That left Senegal knowing they had only to beat Namibia by a

> Khalilou Fadiga once toyed with the idea of playing for Belgium

single goal to qualify for the World Cup on goal difference. They ended up bagging five.

THE KEY PLAYER

Like many of Senegal's stars, playmaker **Khalilou Fadiga** has spent more of his life in France than anywhere else. He left his native country at the age of six and kicked his first ball on the back-streets of Paris.

His first taste of professional football came in Belgium, where he served as a prolific striker for Mechelen and Lommel, and where he met his wife. That made him eligible to play for Belgium – a fact not lost on then national-coach Georges Leekens, who tried to persuade Fadiga to turn out for the *Diables Rouges*.

After mulling it over for a while, Fadiga stuck with Senegal – even though he knew his chances of appearing at the highest international level would be reduced. Now his loyalty has been rewarded, his game having benefitted from a move to French football with Auxerre, where he has adopted a more withdrawn but still crucial role on the pitch.

THE EMERGING TALENT

Despite being just 21, **El Hadji Douf** looks well on the way to becoming Senegal's most prolific goalscorer of all time. One of three Lens players certain of a place in the country's World Cup squad, Douf already has pace, vision, a cool head in front of goal, and a single-mindedness which sometimes results in his team-mates being denied an easier chance.

Douf has something of a bad-boy image away from football, but there are signs he is becoming more focused since moving to Lens from Rennes in the summer of 2001. Meanwhile, his scoring ability remains unquestionable – of the 15 goals Senegal scored in qualifying, nine were his.

THE DUGOUT

Though German-born Peter Schnittger laid some of the groundwork, it is Frenchman **Bruno Metsu** who takes the bulk of the credit for turning Senegal from also-rans into World Cup material.

Formerly a journeyman player and coach in Belgium and northern France, the 48-year-old Metsu specialises in making teams more than the sum of their parts. With Senegal, as at the likes of Lille, Sédan and Valenciennes, he has emphasised physicality and work-rate above all – with impressive, if not always attractive, results.

URUGUAY

URUGUAY One of football's most significant powers is to grace the World Cup or the first time in 12 years. A small country which has had a huge influence on the development of the game, Uruguay would play at every tournament if past achievements were the sole criterion. Yet the fact that the Uruguayans have been absent for so long says much about the attitude of their footballing hierarchy. Rarely lacking in talent, the national side spent much of the 1990s being overshadowed by other South American teams with less of a pedigree but more of a heart. This World Cup represents an opportunity for Uruguay to change all that.

THE PEDIGREE On the back of gold-medal wins at the 1924 and 1928 Olympic Games, **Uruguay** won the right to host the first-ever World Cup in 1930. It was a low-key affair and home soil – as it would prove on numerous further occasions – was the deciding factor, the Uruguayans beating Argentina 4–2 in the final.

More impressive was the team's second triumph, in **Brazil** two decades later, when a team inspired by Juan Alberto Schiaffino defied a crowd of 200,000 inside Rio's Maracana stadium to beat the hosts 2–1 in the deciding game.

In the modern era, a series of teams – the best led by the elegant Enzo Francescoli – have promised much on paper, only to have their potential crushed by arrogance, negative tactics, or a combination of the two.

THE ROAD TO JAPAN/KOREA South America's marathon qualifying programme tends to work as a leveller, and the Uruguayans did well to hang on to the fifth place they occupied when their Argentine-born coach, Daniel Passarella, quit midway through the 18-game campaign.

Passarella's successor, Victor Pua, resisted the temptation to tinker with the line-up, preferring to let class acts such as Juventus defender **Paolo Montero**, Roma midfielder **Gianni Guigou** and young Málaga striker **Darío Silva** continue to dictate the play. A string of vital goals from Silva – not least in a nervy last 1–1 draw at home to Argentina, who had already qualified – were enough to earn Uruguay the dubious pleasure of a two-leg play-off against Australia.

With all the other berths already filled, the eyes of the world were on the tie. A first-leg penalty allowed the Aussies to take a 1–0 lead to the second leg in Montevideo, but Uruguay were unfazed by the media hype surrounding their opponents and, indeed, seemed to revel in the unaccustomed role of underdog. Silva's early goal settled the nerves, then a **Richard Morales** double sent the crowd wild – rekindling, in the process, the spirit of an earlier, more glorious era.

THE KEY PLAYER
When **Alvaro Recoba** arrived in Milan to play for Inter in 1997, nobody took much notice. The media were obsessed with Ronaldo, and the Uruguayan forward was left to his own devices. The lack of fuss suited Recoba, who overcame a loan spell at Venezia, a suspension for having false papers and a series of niggling injuries to claim a regular place in the Inter first team.

At international level, Recoba was fortunate that his suspension applied only to domestic Italian football and allowed him to carry on playing for Uruguay – maintaining his match fitness and, crucially, earning the trust of national coach Victor Pua in his ability to make and take goals with a style that has prompted comparisons with the great Francescoli...

THE EMERGING TALENT
Though still to prove himself at club level since his transfer to Juventus in January 2000, young goalkeeper **Fabian Carini** is very much Uruguay's No 1. A veteran of the Under-19 team which current coach Victor Pua took to the World Youth Cup in 1997,

Carini's relationship with coach Pua goes back to 1997's World Youth Cup

Carini made the step up to full international honours with ease, pulling off a string of vital saves during Uruguay's World Cup qualifying campaign.

THE DUGOUT
As humble and sensitive as some of his predecessors have been brash and arrogant, **Victor Pua** has spent most of his coaching career in the service of the Uruguayan FA. A much-publicised bust-up with striker Darío Silva notwithstanding, Pua has an enviable rapport with his players – but whether his favoured tactic of keeping the lid on expectations works at the highest level remains to be seen.

PARAGUAY

When host nation France came up against the Paraguayans in the second round of the last World Cup, it produced one of the tournament's most memorable matches. Paraguay's dogged resistance, in the face of a pumped-up Lens crowd, was broken only by Laurent Blanc's 113th-minute goal; the look of despair on the visitors' faces said it all. The extraordinary thing is that, four years on, this tiny, impoverished South American nation has produced an even better side – one capable not just of frustrating their opponents, but of outscoring them.

THE PEDIGREE

Prior to their exploits in France four years ago, the Paraguayans had made only one modern-era World Cup appearance – in **Mexico** in 1986, where they came through a very weak first-round group and were then beaten 3–0 by a Gary Lineker-inspired England.

In earlier World Cup history, Paraguay were present at both the 1930 and 1950 tournaments, but failed to win a match at either. They eventually broke their duck in **Sweden** in 1958, recovering from a 7–3 thrashing at the hands of France to draw 3–3 with Yugoslavia and beat Scotland 3–2.

Nothing, however, could compare with the France '98 campaign, when the Paraguayans qualified for the second round ahead of Spain and Bulgaria, their rock-solid defence organised by inspirational goalkeeper and captain José-Luis Chilavert.

Chilavert has appealed against his two-game World Cup suspension

THE ROAD TO JAPAN/KOREA

Paraguay's qualifying campaign began slowly but got a shot in the arm at just the right moment – a 2–1 win over Brazil in Asuncion in July 2000, which acted as the springboard for a seven-game unbeaten run. With **José Cardozo** and **Roque Santa Cruz** (see below) giving the team more attacking options than they'd possessed at France '98, the Paraguayans even began scoring freely, putting three past Venezuela and five past a hapless Peru. Just as importantly, the side also managed to draw home and away with the qualifying group's runaway winners, Argentina.

Defeats in the last two games by Colombia and Venezuela blotted the copy-book, but the Paraguayans had already booked their World Cup tickets by then; they finished fourth in the mini-league table, level on points with Brazil.

THE KEY PLAYER
Whether **José-Luis Chilavert** can make as big an impact on this World Cup as on the last will depend on the outcome of an appeal against his suspension for the first two fixtures. Accused of spitting at Brazil's Roberto Carlos last year, Chilavert may yet be forced to sit out Paraguay's games with South Africa and Spain.

For the sake of spectacle, if nothing else, that would be a shame. As good a shot-stopper as there is anywhere in the world, Chilavert is one of goalkeeping's true extroverts, stepping up to take not just penalties but fearsome long-range free-kicks (while one of his much put-upon defenders scurries back to cover on the line).

A topsy-turvy club career has seen him win the Copa Libertadores with Argentina's Velez Sarsfield and, most recently, inspire lowly Racing Strasbourg to victory in the 2001 French Cup.

THE EMERGING TALENT
If one man sums up the difference between the current Paraguay line-up and the 1998 vintage, it's **Roque Santa Cruz.** A virtual unknown when Bayern Munich signed him in 1999, he has gone on to become a useful performer for both club and country, despite not yet having turned 21.

At Bayern Santa Cruz is often used as a 'super-sub' to add fresh impetus in the latter stages of key *Bundesliga* or Champions' League ties. For Paraguay he is a regular starter, justifying his selection with three World Cup qualifying goals and a string of assists.

THE DUGOUT
Following Sergio Makarian's inexplicable sacking eight days after Paraguay had qualified for the World Cup, **Cesare Maldini** has taken over the coaching reins. He has all the relevant experience, having led Italy in France four years ago. Perhaps more importantly, Chilavert approves of his appointment.

SLOVENIA

Unbeaten in competitive football since Spain edged them 2–1 at Euro 2000, the Slovenes are nobody's fools. To qualify for a second successive major tournament is no mean feat for a country with a population of less than two million, where none of the football grounds can hold more than 20,000 fans. But to pigeonhole Slovenia as a 'plucky little nation' with no hope of troubling the World Cup's bigger teams is to under-estimate the squad's potential – not least the extent to which it has improved over the past two years.

THE PEDIGREE

Part of Yugoslavia until 1991, Slovenia has a good excuse for its lack of World Cup history. Yet the republic was often (rightly) viewed as the corner of Yugoslavia least capable of producing footballing talent.

As a consequence, Slovene-born players only occasionally featured in Yugoslav World Cup squads. Brane Oblak made it into the 1974 line-up in **West Germany**, while current coach Srecko Katanec played in midfield for Yugoslavia at **Italia '90**. And that's about it.

THE ROAD TO JAPAN/KOREA

If Slovenia's path to Euro 2000 was made smoother by a weak qualifying group, the route to their first World Cup was always going to be rockier. Russia, Yugoslavia and Switzerland all had superior resources, and when the Slovenes conceded two goals in the last three minutes against the Faroe Isles in their opening game, the omens were not good.

As before, though, Slovenia rose to the big occasion. The Swiss were beaten in Basle; a late penalty saw off the Russians in Ljubljana; and the Yugoslavs came no closer to beating their former countrymen than they had at Euro 2000.

Russia having won the group, Slovenia beat the Faroes at home to secure second place and a play-off against Romania. **Milenko Acimovic**, a habitual scorer of vital goals, and **Milan Osterc** did the damage as the Slovenes overcame a 1–0 deficit to win the home leg 2–1, after which Portsmouth's **Mladen Rudonja** chose the return in which to end a 52-game goalless streak for his country, taking his team into a 3–1 aggregate lead which the Romanians halved but could not eliminate.

For the Slovenes, history had repeated itself – they had qualified for Euro 2000 by beating Ukraine with the same combination of results.

THE KEY PLAYER

An unlikely hero at Euro 2000, **Zlatko Zahovic** may have his work cut out to make a similar impact on the World Cup. His talents as both a maker and scorer of crucial goals are not in doubt, and he remains a cult-hero in Slovenia despite never having played club football there. Yet injury ruled him

The relationship between coach and star has recently come under strain

out of the vital play-off against Romania, and his absence was barely felt.

More worryingly, Zahovic has since incurred the wrath of coach Srecko Katanec with his apparent reluctance to fit friendly internationals into his schedule. After disastrous spells in Greek and Spanish football, the player is trying to revive his fading club career in Portugal with Benfica.

Despite all this, Zahovic is certain to be selected for Japan/Korea, if only because no other Slovene can match his improvisational skills.

THE EMERGING TALENT

Slovenian footballer of the year in 2000/01, **Nastja Ceh** has since moved from Maribor to Club Bruges of Belgium, and shows every sign of maturing into a midfielder of real class. A late developer, the 24-year-old Ceh didn't receive a full international call-up until the last game of Slovenia's qualifying group programme – and responded with the first two goals in a 3–0 win over the Faroe Isles.

Like the established Zahovic, with whom comparisons are already being made, Ceh is at his most dangerous playing just behind the front players, where his smart close control and thunderous left-foot shot come into their own.

THE DUGOUT

Another living legend of Slovene football, **Srecko Katanec** became national-team coach in July 1998. His players haven't looked back since, taking their cue from his unshakeable belief, his meticulous attention to detail and, above all, his tireless enthusiasm.

SOUTH AFRICA
Still the African nation with the greatest football potential, still showing only fitful signs that it can be realised on the world stage, the *Bafana Bafana* are an enigma which is not going to be resolved anytime soon. The rehabilitation of the country's footballers after the wilderness years of apartheid couldn't have got off to a more vibrant start, South Africa winning the African Nations Cup as hosts in 1996. Yet the matchless team spirit and enthusiasm which inspired that victory quickly evaporated. Without it, the South Africans look likely to remain mavericks in today's increasingly disciplined and professional footballing environment.

THE PEDIGREE
For decades, South Africa were banned from taking part in international football – the inevitable consequence of sporting sanctions against the country's hated apartheid regime.

After that regime was dismantled during the early 1990s, the world welcomed the new, multi-cultural face of South African football. A richly talented, mixed-race team, the so-called *Bafana Bafana*, built on their 1996 African Nations Cup success by qualifying for **France '98** in style. Yet once at the finals, the South Africans' discipline deserted them. They went home early after scarcely troubling their first-round group opponents France, Denmark and Saudi Arabia, beginning a period of turbulence for the local game – prolonged by the shock defeat of South Africa's bid to host the 2006 World Cup.

THE ROAD TO JAPAN/KOREA
After beating Lesotho home and away to qualify for the group stages, South Africa began a campaign that was to be dogged by controversy. Their first game, away to Zimbabwe in Harare, had to be abandoned after police fired teargas on fans, causing a stampede in which 13 people were killed. The match was awarded to South Africa, who had been 2–0 up with seven minutes left.

Six months later, a useful-looking Guinea side (who the South Africans had yet to face) were expelled from the group because of alleged political interference, their unbeaten record being considered null and void by FIFA. Finally, Malawi appealed unsuccessfully that their 2–1 home defeat by South Africa should be replayed, after the visiting team swapped hotels and stayed in the same lodgings as the match officials, in contravention of FIFA rules.

Despite all this, it is hard to argue against South Africa's record of five wins in six games. **Delron Buckley**, scorer of both goals in the ill-fated Zimbabwe game, and **Sibusiso Zuma** used the qualifiers to establish themselves as first-team regulars, giving the old guard of **Phil Masinga** and **Shaun Bartlett** a run for their money in attack.

THE KEY PLAYER After being appointed South Africa's captain in place of the often injured or otherwise unavailable Lucas Radebe, **Shaun Bartlett** has more on his plate than ever. Can he lead his team from the front? The omens are good. A late developer, Bartlett has risen to the challenge of playing Premiership football with Charlton, despite having spent much of his career in the obscurity of America's MLS and the Swiss league.

Bartlett's broad knowledge of the game will be useful

Barlett's long and varied career gives him a broad understanding of the game – one which may be tested to the full by in-fighting within the *Bafana Bafana* during this World Cup.

THE EMERGING TALENT Of all the players to make the breakthrough into South Africa's first team since the last World Cup, **Sibusisu Zuma** has been arguably the most consistent. Though not the most prolific of goalscorers, he boasts a strong physical presence, great awareness and a useful turn of speed – attributes which have served him well at his club, FC Copenhagen.

Zuma will be 27 during the World Cup, but still looks to have a bright future ahead of him, regardless of South Africa's results.

THE DUGOUT The man who nurtured Portugal's current 'golden generation' in the early 1990s, **Carlos Queiroz** has a very different task in taking South Africa to Japan/Korea. Whereas his Portuguese youngsters were keen to learn as a group, his latest charges have proved much harder to manage – and he is running out of time in which to make a difference.

SPAIN

If any other nation had been among the first to qualify for a World Cup, with six wins in eight games, 21 goals scored and just four conceded, expectations within its footballing community would soar. But this is Spain, and its people have been here before. The Spanish may have a domestic league that is now unquestionably the strongest in the world; they may have a team capable of making the current World Cup holders look ordinary (as Spain did in a friendly last year). But under-achievement has been the name of Spain's game so many times in the past, it seems foolish to predict that history will not repeat itself.

THE PEDIGREE

While the giants of Real Madrid and Barcelona have often dominated club football, the national side has seldom looked capable of similar supremacy. Spain's best World Cup performance came in **Brazil** in 1950, when they finished fourth in a group-based final stage.

In the modern era, the Spaniards exited in the second round when they themselves hosted the World Cup in 1982 – though not before a goalless draw in their last game had also eliminated England. A less inhibited, more expansive style of football was played by the class of **USA '94**, until their progress was controversially halted by Italy in the quarter-finals.

Four years ago in **France**, Javier Clemente's side were among the pre-tournament favourites but never recovered from losing their opening game to Nigeria, and went home before the knockout stage.

THE ROAD TO JAPAN/KOREA

Not for the first time, the Spaniards enjoyed the luck of the qualifying draw. José Antonio Camacho's side had finished Euro 2000 on something of a high, having started with customary inertia, then rallied to beat Slovenia and Yugoslavia before losing narrowly to the all-conquering French. Now the likes of Austria, Israel and Bosnia-Hercegovina were no match

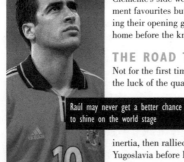

Raúl may never get a better chance to shine on the world stage

for an already useful team, further bolstered by the arrival of **Gerard**, **Iván Helguera**, **Ruben Baraja** and **Diego Tristán**, among others.

It was Tristán who got the ball rolling in the 4–0 home win over Austria which guaranteed Spain's top-place finish on 1 September 2001 – while the rest of Europe was still battling it out for a World Cup berth.

THE KEY PLAYER
He's been around for so long that it seems inconceivable he is still only 24. Yet when you're **Raúl González Blanco** and you were the youngest player ever to turn out for the Real Madrid first team at the age of 17 years and four months, time doesn't always fly by the way it does for the rest of football.

Yet despite his tender years, Raúl may never get a better chance to shine on the global stage than at the 2002 World Cup. His own game has continued to mature alongside that of his international team-mates, and with Spain not having been drawn in the toughest of first-round groups, the way should be clear for a good, solid run in the tournament.

To predict such an outcome, though, would be to tempt fate in a way that Raúl – like all Spanish players of his generation – is reluctant to do.

THE EMERGING TALENT
One of many youngsters to be given his first taste of international football by José-Antonio Camacho, **Juan Carlos Valeron** revels in any number of midfield roles. Unspectacular but dependable, Valeron would arguably have been more at home in the disciplined teams fashioned by Camacho's predecessor, Javier Clemente. Yet his constant prompting and probing have been gleefully seized upon by Spain's legions of eager young forwards – never more so than during the qualifying competition for Japan/Korea.

A graduate of Hector Cúper's ground-breaking Mallorca side in the late 1990s, Valeron had the misfortune to be sold to Atlético Madrid just at the point when the latter club was about to hit its great financial crisis. Since the summer of 2000 he has been at Deportivo La Coruña.

THE DUGOUT
A former captain of both Real Madrid and Spain, and a coach of the former, **José-Antonio Camacho** has become that great rarity – a popular Spanish national coach. The players love his emphasis on attack; the fans love his willingness to try out new talents; the press love his accommodating attitude. Is it a winning combination?

BRAZIL

'Basically, they look like a pub side.' That was the verdict of one British pundit who travelled to Rio to watch Brazil struggle through the qualifying stages for this year's World Cup. He was exaggerating, of course, but the very fact that such a comment could be made without being greeted with derision tells you all you need to know about the Brazilians' build-up to the finals. Seasoned Brazil-watchers are comparing the current situation with that of 1974, when Mario Zagallo's team ended up trying to muscle their way to the trophy – and failed. Others reckon the current squad is too talented to suffer such a fate, while conceding that the way forward is far from obvious. What everyone can agree on, though, is that Brazil have fallen an implausibly long way from the heights they scaled at the last World Cup, four short years ago.

THE PEDIGREE

Where to start? Brazil didn't contest a World Cup final until 1950 when, as the host nation, they were surprisingly beaten by Uruguay in the final match in Rio. Eight years later, in **Sweden**, the emergence of a 17-year-old by the name of Pelé gave an already richly talented side the inspiration it needed to lift the trophy, the home side being defeated 5–2 in an exhilirating final.

Four years later, in **Chile**, the Brazilians retained the Cup after beating a slightly unlucky Czechoslovakia 3–1 in the final. And while England were to take centre-stage in 1966, Pelé returned to the fore at **Mexico '70**, leading arguably the greatest band of Brazilians (including Tostão, Jairzinho and skipper Carlos Alberto) to a record-breaking third World Cup, their 4–1 trouncing of Italy in the final being a performance of such sublime style, its like may never be seen again.

After the low point of 1974, Brazil returned to form but, despite fielding a series of outstanding talents such as Zico, Falcão, Júnior and Sócrates, the World Cups of 1978, '82 and '86 were destined for other hands. A young Romário had the world talking in 1990 and, while his team made a premature exit from that competition, they won their reward at **USA '94**, albeit in disappointing circumstances, thanks to a shoot-out victory over Italy in a goalless final.

Brazil reached the final again four years ago and, once again, failed to score in it. The exact circumstances surrounding Ronaldo's poor performance against France may never be known – but Brazil did enough in the rest of the tournament to win over a new generation of fans.

THE ROAD TO JAPAN/KOREA Four coaches, 18 games and 63 players after they'd begun their World Cup qualifying campaign, Brazil finally assured themselves of a place in the finals with a 3–0 win at home to Venezuela. It was a reflection of how bad things had become that the Brazilian FA claimed special dispensation to move the fixture to the tiny town of São Luis – away from the cat-calls of Rio and São Paulo.

As if the pain of the qualifiers were not deep enough, in between them Brazil managed to lose all face on the international stage, being dumped out of the 2000 Olympic football tournament by Cameroon (resulting in the departure of Coach No 1, Wanderley Luxemburgo); losing to Australia in the 2001 Confederations Cup (exit Emerson Leão); and, worst of all, going down 2–0 to Honduras in quarter-finals of the Copa America – a result which the current coach, Luiz Felipe Scolari, somehow managed to survive.

THE KEY PLAYER Consistent performers have been few and far between for Brazil these past two years, but at least **Rivaldo** has generally got the job done. Overshadowed by Ronaldo at France '98, he succeeded his compatriot at Barcelona and is now widely regarded as a more complete – not to mention much less injury-prone – performer.

Matchless dribbling skills, superb vision and a whole menu of fancy flicks are all Rivaldo's stock in trade, but the 30-year-old forward's eight goals in qualifying have been his greatest contribution to the cause.

THE EMERGING TALENT Brazil's ability to generate new talent is never in doubt, but such has been the state of flux in the national side in recent times, it has been hard for any player to make a genuine breakthrough. One exception to this rule is AC Milan defender **Roque Júnior**, whose keen positional sense and uncompromising tackling have seen him survive three changes of coach.

THE DUGOUT Those who fear a repeat of 1974 point the finger at **Luiz Felipe Scolari**, a self-confessed admirer of defensive football who has publicly played down the achievements of Brazil between 1958 and 1970. A journeyman player who has been successful as a coach at club level, Scolari has insisted that his tactics were necessary to bring stability to the national side. Whether they will bring glory is a moot point – as is the question of whether he will get the chance to try them out in the finals.

CHINA

CHINA The world's most populous nation, its economy thriving and its standard of living soaring, has fallen in love with football. Now, at last, it has the chance to follow its national team at the planet's greatest football tournament. The consequences should be exciting, if impossible to forecast accurately. For, enthusiastic and influential as they may be, the Chinese are still at an early stage when it comes to football development. The nation's domestic competition, the C-League, has been running for only a few years and was recently struck by scandal, when a number of referees admitted taking bribes to swing matches. Internationally, too, China are novices with everything to prove – so much so that it has taken a journeyman coach from former Yugoslavia to lead them to their first World Cup in the face of enormous public and media pressure.

THE PEDIGREE There isn't one, of course. As recently as 1986, China were being eliminated from the World Cup qualifying tournament by a Hong Kong side run by British expat former pros.

> Fan Zhiyi's first World Cup will probably be his last

Progress after that was steady but not as rapid as the Chinese football authorities had hoped. In Asia's often convoluted qualifying programmes, smaller but more accomplished Arab sides kept getting in China's way – Iraq in the run-up to the 1994 tournament, Qatar four years later.

Away from the World Cup, the Chinese can point to a semi-final placing at the last Asian Cup finals in Lebanon – but, again, it was an accomplishment that was a long time in coming.

THE ROAD TO JAPAN/KOREA Despite the arrival of Bora Milutinovic (see below) as coach, China began the qualifying process hesitantly. Their first-round group contained genuine international minnows such as Cambodia and the Maldives, yet the Chinese struggled to impose themselves, winning only 1–0 away to the latter after knocking ten past them at home.

Even so, it was with a 100% record that China progressed to the second round where, by common consent, they were allocated the easier of the two groups, alongside the UAE, Uzbekistan, Qatar and Oman. They sustained only one defeat in eight games – 1–0 away to the Uzbeks – and that was after they'd already assured themselves of a first-ever World Cup place with a 3–0 win over the nation that had denied the Chinese four years ago, Qatar.

THE KEY PLAYER

One of the first of China's footballing exports to Europe **Fan Zhiyi** is a former captain of the national side and, at the age of 32, remains its central defensive linchpin.

Fan's bulky, muscular frame was first seen in the colours of Crystal Palace, who bought him and his compatriot Sun Jihai (see below) from Shanghai Shenhua for a combined transfer fee of £1million in 1998. While Sun soon returned to China, Fan remained at Palace until October 2001, when he was sold to Dundee.

Wherever he plays, though, Fan puts his commanding stature to good use, dominating the centre of defence with surprising elegance, and also coming forward at set pieces to some effect. He scored four times during China's World Cup qualifying campaign, two of the goals being penalties.

THE EMERGING TALENT

While **Sun Jihai** may not have lasted the pace of English football as well as his former captain, the fact that Kevin Keegan recently expressed an interest in bringing him to Maine Road is an indication of how much the 24-year-old midfielder has improved since his return to China.

Though not as formidable a physical presence as Fan Zhiyi, Sun has superior pace and is more flexible. He prefers a central, playmaking role but is versatile enough to be used on either flank – where China coach Bora Milutinovic often put him during the qualifiers.

THE DUGOUT

A softly spoken, 57-year-old Croatian who will be at his fifth successive World Cup with a fifth different team, **Bora Milutinovic** is the footballing firefighter *par excellence*. Expert at taking under-performing teams to a higher level, his previous charges were Mexico (1986), Costa Rica (1990), the USA (1994) and Nigeria (1998). His verdict on 2002? "China have won the World Cup just by qualifying."

COSTA RICA

Often described as a haven of stability in a politically volatile region, Costa Rica is the only Central American nation which can rival Mexico for footballing strength. The difference between the two is that while Mexican teams invariably have to struggle under the weight of immense public expectation, the Costa Ricans are under no pressure – with the US, Canada and a string of emerging Caribbean nations also in the hunt, to qualify for the World Cup at all is deemed a triumph in itself.

THE PEDIGREE

The Costa Ricans' only previous World Cup finals appearance was at **Italia '90**, where they began as the tournament's rank outsiders. A team of complete unknowns who seemed to have arrived at the finals almost by accident, they left Scotland and Sweden dazed by their idiosyncratic, counter-attacking football, beating both (and also giving Brazil a decent game) to defy the sceptics and qualify for the second round. There they were well-beaten by Czechoslovakia, but not before squandering a couple of chances which could have turned the game.

Away from the World Cup, the Costa Ricans are regular participants at the CONCACAF Gold Cup – though they have never won it. They finished runners-up to the US in this year's tournament.

THE ROAD TO JAPAN/KOREA

Qualifying for the World Cup from the CONCACAF region is never a straightforward business, and Costa Rica certainly made a meal of things this time around. Despite being seeded – thereby avoiding the first qualifying round – the *Ticos* still contrived to lose to Barbados and Guatemala, and indeed only qualified for the final round after a play-off with the latter in Miami.

In the final group stage, however, the Costa Ricans found their rhythm, chalking up home-and-away wins over Jamaica and a first-ever victory in Mexico, and losing only once – to the US in Kansas City. They finished top of the group, six points clear of the pack and with the nation partying like it was 1990.

THE KEY PLAYER

Sole survivor of the class of 1990 and a fully fledged folk-hero to boot, **Hernán Medford** is expected to roll back the years in Japan/Korea as Costa Rica set about trying to repeat – or even exceed – their achievements of 12 years ago. In Italy Medford was an out-

and-out target man, with impressive acceleration and a towering, intimidating frame. He scored the goal that beat Sweden and took Costa Rica into the second round, and his name has been synonymous with the national team ever since.

These days Medford plays in a more withdrawn role, but his influence is just as great – it was his goal that ended Mexico's decades-old unbeaten run at the Azteca stadium during qualifying.

The 34-year-old Medford will earn his 80th cap during the finals and will celebrate 17 years of service to the Costa Rican national setup, having first represented his country at the World Youth Cup of 1985.

THE EMERGING TALENT
Though he is an established figure within English club football, **Paulo Wanchope** is only now gaining a proper international stage on which to parade his unqiue talents.

Wanchope's unpredictable game sums up the Costa Rican style

Like the Costa Rica of Italia '90, Wanchope was a complete unknown when Jim Smith brought him and his compatriot Mauricio Solis to Derby County in 1997. Yet Wanchope made an immediate impact with two goals on his debut against Manchester United. Now at Manchester City, he has survived a spell on the transfer list and a series of injuries to earn himself a place in the hearts of the Maine Road faithful.

Yet the best showcase for his unique, rapid-fire style of football may yet turn out to be the national side, for whom Wanchope scored seven goals during qualifying.

THE DUGOUT
Brazilian-born **Alexandre Guimarães** was named Costa Rica coach on the eve of the team's vital qualifying play-off against Guatemala in January 2001. His impact was immediate. Switching to the counter-attacking style that had served the country so well in 1990, Guimarães saw his side win 5–2. They never looked back, and with players such as Paulo Wanchope revelling in the long, early, diagonal ball the coach has prescribed, Costa Rica have a new confidence about them as they approach the World Cup.

TURKEY

The World Cup could not have come at a better time for the Turks. The achievements of two years ago – when the national side reached the second round of Euro 2000 and Galatasaray became the first Turkish club to win a European trophy – are there to be built on, and the squad looks more than capable. While most of the side continues to play in Turkish club football, an increasing number are now earning their living abroad, dispelling the myth that Turks don't travel well – and gaining useful new experience into the bargain.

THE PEDIGREE

Surprisingly, given Turkey's progress since they qualified for Euro '96, this will be the country's first World Cup of the modern era. Their only previous appearance came in **Switzerland** in 1954, where they beat Korea 7–0 but contrived to lose twice to eventual winners West Germany, the first time 4–1, the second (in a group-deciding play-off) 7–2. Four years earlier, they had actually qualified for the finals by beating Syria 7–0, but withdrew at the last minute.

The 1960s, '70s and '80s were bleak years for the Turkish game. As recently as 1986, the Turks finished bottom of their qualifying group, without a win in eight games, and with England having put 13 goals past them. Such grim statistics would be unthinkable now.

THE ROAD TO JAPAN/KOREA

Turkey spent the early part of the qualifying programme looking a safe bet for top spot in a diverse but not overly taxing group that also contained Sweden, Slovakia, Macedonia, Moldova and Azerbaijan. But a surprising 2–1 home defeat by Sweden, in which the visitors scored twice in the last three minutes, handed the initiative to the Scandinavians.

A 3–0 win in Moldova was enough for second place, though, and a berth in the play-offs, where Turkey drew Austria. It looked an uneven contest on paper, and so it proved. **Okan Buruk**'s strike on the hour in Vienna gave the Turks a single-goal advantage to take home, but there was to be no resting on laurels in Istanbul four days later, where Buruk was again on the scoresheet in a 5–0 romp.

THE KEY PLAYER

A familiar face on the European football scene for the best part of a decade, **Hakan Sükür** is only now gaining the widespread acclaim his talents deserve. Always an idol in his native

Turkey, where he is nicknamed the 'Bull of the Bosphorus', Hakan spent much of the late '90s trying to repair the damage to his international reputation done by a disastrous move from Galatasaray to Torino in 1995. He played just five games before returning to Istanbul suffering from homesickness. Was this proof that Turkish footballers couldn't take the pressure of the bigger leagues?

Five years later, Hakan himself answered that question by helping Gala to the UEFA Cup and Turkey to the second round of Euro 2000. Inter were so impressed that when Ronaldo reported sick for the start of another season, they signed Hakan. He has remained with the Milan club ever since, and while some of the old speed has gone from his game, Hakan's eye for goal remains as sharp as ever – he scored one and made a further two in Turkey's 5–0 trouncing of Austria.

THE EMERGING TALENT A

former team-mate of Hakan's at Galatasaray, **Hasan Sas** is the man Turkey's strikers increasingly look to for telling crosses and through balls.

Not a natural goalscorer himself, Hasan seems happy enough providing the ammunition for others, his pace and skill on the ball proving a threat to any opposing full-back. And, unlike many wide men, he enjoys tackling back – a little too much so at times.

Hasan's pace and ingenuity pose a threat to any full-back

Like many of his generation he has been targeted by several west European clubs, and is expected to join Nantes after the World Cup.

THE DUGOUT Once upon a time the Turks relied on foreign
coaches to manage their national team. But **Senol Gunes** became the third successive Turk to be given the job when he took over from Mustafa Denizli after Euro 2000. A former international defender whose main playing and coaching successes came with provincial club Trabzonspor, he is already beginning to enjoy the same levels of respect accorded to the architect of Turkey's great footballing renaissance, Fatih Terim.

POLAND

This grand old name from the World Cup's classic past is returning to the finals after a 16-year absence – and even the Poles themselves seem surprised by their team's revival. Two years ago, it was Poland's failure to take a point from their last qualifier in Sweden which allowed England a back-door pass to Euro 2000 via the play-offs. Today, the dearth of confidence and ideas which characterised that Polish line-up have been swept aside and, if the run of the ball goes their way, Poland could spring yet more surprises before the 2002 World Cup is out.

THE PEDIGREE

Poland did not make any real impact on the World Cup until the 1974 tournament in **West Germany**. Having eliminated England in qualifying, a classic line-up containing goalkeeper Jan Tomaszewski, playmaker Kazimierz Deyna and striker Grzegorz Lato went all the way to the semi-finals before losing narrowly to the hosts.

In **Argentina** four years later Poland were even stronger, their attacking options strengthened by Zbigniew Boniek, arguably the quickest and most extravagantly talented forward of his generation. Alas, the team's lyrical approach to the game was no match for the physicality of the host nation in the second round.

At **Spain '82**, Boniek was suspended for the semi-final against Italy, and the nation again had to be content with remaining one step away from the final. Poland's presence in Spain was accompanied by demonstrations in aid of the *Solidarity* movement, and by the time Gary Lineker was eliminating a weaker Polish side from Mexico '86, the country was being ruled by martial law.

THE ROAD TO JAPAN/KOREA

History shows that *Solidarity* eventually triumphed. Yet while Poland's political and economic liberalisation might have been good for many of its people, it was not good for its football. The 1990s were the Poles' World Cup wilderness years, and there was little hope of a recovery as the qualifying phase for 2002 kicked-off.

Yet new coach Jerzy Engel, fielding a largely inexperienced side comprising mainly home-based players, saw his youngsters start with a 3–1 win over Ukraine in Kiev. Soon Belarus and a much-fancied Norway had also been beaten, and when once stopper **Tomasz Hajto** had returned to central defence alongside his Schalke team-mate **Tomasz Waldoch**, there was no stopping Poland. Qualification as group winners was assured on 1 September 2001, with a 3–0 trouncing of Norway in Chorzów.

THE KEY PLAYER While the presence of Hajto, Waldoch and national player of the year Jerzy Dudek make Poland solid in defence, it is **Emmanuel Olisadebe** who can claim most credit for putting the country back on the World Cup map.

A 23-year-old Nigerian whose application for Polish citizenship was rushed through by officials, Olisadebe scored three minutes into his debut in Kiev and hasn't looked back since. His exhilarating pace and predatory instincts in front of goal are contrasted by an almost self-effacing attitude off the pitch, which resulted in him expressing sympathy for Polish fans who greeted him with racist abuse – "they weren't used to seeing

Olisadebe chose Poland ahead of his native Nigeria

black people." Olisadebe now plays in Greece with Panathinaikos, but the signs are that his heart remains very much with his adopted homeland.

THE EMERGING TALENT Despite averaging almost a goal a game for Polish champions Wisla Kraków in the first part of the 2001/02 season, **Maciej Zurawski** played no part in the World Cup qualifying campaign. Yet he received a call-up into an experimental squad for warm-up games in February and remains hopeful that if he can maintain his scoring form at club level, he will get his chance in Japan/Korea.

THE DUGOUT Having uncovered the talents of Olisadebe and inspired the run-down railway workers' club Polonia Warsaw to the league title, **Jerzy Engel** adopted a typically novel approach to his new job as national coach in 1999. Encouraging his players to revel in the role of underdog, rather than trade on past glories, he reaped instant rewards and was named Poland's coach of the year for 2001. Time will tell whether the same methods work on a grander stage.

PORTUGAL
Seconds away from taking France to a shoot-out in the semi-finals of Euro 2000 and now preparing to host the next edition of the European Championship, Portugal have yet to prove that their distinctive, almost romantic brand of football can thrive on the world stage. The current 'Golden Generation' of players, many of whom have been together since winning the World Under-21 Championship on home soil 11 years ago, has a better chance of proving the point than any since the Eusébio-inspired class of '66. Yet the suspicion remains that in order to really make their mark, the Portuguese will have to sacrifice some of the style which has endeared them to so many for so long.

THE PEDIGREE
It was Eusébio, a Mozambique-born forward of prodigious speed and shooting power, who led Portugal to their first World Cup finals appearance in **England** in 1966. Once there his team broke Brazil's stranglehold on the trophy by knocking them out of the group stage; came back from three down to beat North Korea 5–3 in a classic quarter-final at Goodison Park; and were beaten only by two brilliant Bobby Charlton strikes in their semi against the hosts at Wembley.

Portugal would wait two decades for another chance to shine at the global level, and when it came, at **Mexico '86**, the squad that had so distinguished itself at the European Championship two years earlier fell into disarray in an argument over appearance money. After a 3–1 defeat by Morocco in their final group game, the Portuguese were packing their bags.

Since then, Portugal have saved their best for their own continent, their stylish progress halted by Karel Poborsky's chip for the Czech Republic in the quarter-finals of Euro '96, and by Abel Xavier's handball on the line against the French in that semi two years ago.

THE ROAD TO JAPAN/KOREA
Portugal had the misfortune to be thrown into difficult World Cup qualifying sections for most of the 1990s, and the 2002 event was no exception. Yet a squad containing **Luís Figo**, **Rui Costa**, **Sérgio Conceição** and **João Pinto** approached to so-called 'Group of Death' containing Holland and Ireland with a confidence which was not misplaced.

The Irish held them to a 1–1 draw in Lisbon at the start of October 2000, but within four days Portugal had swept Holland aside with a 2–0 win in Rotterdam – a result which, if anything, flattered the Dutch. The tables were almost turned in the return in Porto the following March, but Figo's last-minute penalty earned Portugal a share of the points, and after that there was no looking back. A 5–0 win over Estonia in their final game was enough for the Portuguese to claim top spot ahead of Ireland on goal difference.

Figo typifies a confidence that has not turned to arrogance

THE KEY PLAYER European footballer of the year in 2000, FIFA world player of the year in 2001, and a man whose contract with Real Madrid guarantees him earnings of more than £15million, **Luís Figo** remains a remarkably down-to-earth figure.

A naturally gifted forward who can score goals from almost anywhere and whose skills make use of the full width of the pitch, Figo is the embodiment of the current Portuguese side. As individually talented as anyone at this World Cup, he is by instinct a team player, his humility honed during his years with Sporting Lisbon and the national Under-21 side under coach and mentor Carlos Queiroz.

Figo celebrates his 30th birthday this year and, while Euro 2004 will be his swansong, Japan/Korea may see his influence at its most telling.

THE EMERGING TALENT For all the team's fine approach play, Portugal's achilles heel has often been the lack of a goal-poacher. **Nuno Gomes**, who gave Portugal the lead against France at Euro 2000, could be that player. A move from Benfica to cash-strapped Fiorentina has not helped his club career, yet his ability to make the most of a small number of chances remains unmatched by any of his countrymen.

THE DUGOUT The man who inspired FC Porto to a succession of fine European runs in the mid-1990s, **António Oliveira** has adopted a typically professional approach to the national-team job since replacing Humberto Coelho after Euro 2000. If anyone can inject the necessary ruthlessness into a side that sometimes appears too nice for its own good, Oliveira is the man.

SOUTH KOREA

The World Cup's co-hosts are a mixed bag. Comfortably Asia's most accomplished performers on the world stage, the Koreans were slow to implement a modern, professional league structure at home. The consequent lack of proven commercial potential was, arguably, the single biggest factor in Korea being obliged to share the World Cup with its arch-rvial Japan, rather than hosting the event outright. Whether the national side can now provide the domestic game with the impetus it needs for further development probably hinges on just one thing – getting as far as the second round.

THE PEDIGREE

After a calamitous first appearance in **Switzerland** in 1954 (and after neighbours North Korea had won political points with their giant-killing antics in England 12 years later), South Korea graced the modern World Cup for the first time at **Mexico '86**. The team managed only a point in their three games (from a dour 1–1 draw with Bulgaria), but the entertaining football the Koreans showed during narrow defeats by Argentina and Italy endeared them to stadium and TV audiences alike.

Korea failed to win a point at **Italia '90** but had their best World Cup yet at **USA '94**, scoring two goals in the last five minutes to force a 2–2 draw with Spain, managing a second draw with Bolivia and losing to Germany 3–2 after going in at half-time three goals down. As in Mexico, the Koreans' refreshingly cavalier approach to the game, coupled with a willingness to shoot on sight from unlikely distances, won them many fans.

At **France '98**, however, South Korea were less impressive, despite being coached by playing legend Cha Bum-keun (a veteran of the '86 campaign) and fielding several players with European and/or J-League playing experience.

They were a goal up in their first game against Mexico but lost 3–1 after playing for an hour with only ten men; were outclassed 5–0 by Holland; then scrapped

Only a second-round placing will bring out the smiles

to a 1–1 draw against Belgium. Cha resigned after the tournament, his countrymen apparently as far from victory in a World Cup match as ever.

THE ROAD TO JAPAN/KOREA

Qualifying for any tournament as a host nation is usually a mixed blessing. The Koreans will not want for noisy and enthusiastic support, but the lack of competitive football will not have done them any favours.

On those occasions since 1998 when they have entered competitive tournaments, South Korea have sent out mixed signals. They reached the semi-finals of the CONCACAF Gold Cup earlier this year, yet scored only twice in four games to get there.

THE KEY PLAYER

South Korea's ability to qualify for the second round of this World Cup may hinge on the form of **Seol Ki-hyeon**. One of the few Korean strikers to possess a real penalty-box presence, Seol has honed his skills in the Belgian league, where the combination of sophisticated tactics and unpredictable playing surfaces requires forwards to be as commanding in the air as they are capable on the ground.

A transfer last summer from Antwerp to Anderlecht has further sharpened Seol's game, and he scored a hat-trick for the Brussels club when they won the Belgian SuperCup in the autumn of 2001. He may yet have another leap to make – both physically and metaphorically – to transfer that kind of form to the World Cup stage.

THE EMERGING TALENT

The pin-up boy of the Korean game, **Ahn Jung-hwan** typifies all that's best about his country's football, coupling clear midfield vision with a tiger-ish attitude. The worry for South Korea is that, since his loan move from Pusan Icons to the *Serie A* club Perugia in the summer of 2000, Ahn has struggled for regular first-team football and may be short of match fitness come May.

THE DUGOUT

It took the Korean FA a long time to come round to the idea of appointing a European coach, and Dutchman **Guus Hiddink** would no doubt argue that 18 months of mainly low-key football is insufficient preparation for such a historic challenge. As might be expected, the Dutch influence has had its impact on the Koreans' shape and tactical awareness – but Hiddink's fear is that the squad still lacks a cutting edge.

UNITED STATES

After the humiliation of finishing last at the 1998 World Cup, the Americans approach this tournament with a younger squad, a widely respected coach and one trophy already in the cabinet, thanks to their triumph in the Gold Cup earlier this year. True, that tournament is open only to members of CONCACAF and invited guests, but the victory was significant because it was achieved by a squad with its roots in Major League Soccer, the domestic championship charged not just with making football a commercial success in the States, but with producing the country's next generation of international stars.

THE PEDIGREE

In the early days of the World Cup, teams of enthusiastic American amateurs made quite an impact on the tournament. The US reached the semi-finals in **Uruguay** in 1930, then beat England 1–0 in the first round of the 1950 tournament in **Brazil**, in what still counts as one of the greatest upsets in World Cup history.

In the modern era, American soccer teams – usually deprived of the lavish incentives available to their counterparts in baseball, basketball or gridiron – have struggled to impose themselves in the same way. The US lost all three of their games at **Italia '90**, and although home advantage gave the team the attention they craved (and deserved) four years later, it also brought unaccustomed pressure; the Americans won only one game out of four, and bowed out to Brazil in the second round.

Things were to get much worse at **France '98**, when a visibly ageing side lost to Germany, Yugoslavia and – most embarrassingly, for political reasons if nothing else – Iran, scoring only a single goal in the process.

THE ROAD TO JAPAN/KOREA

These days, the granting of three World Cup places to the CONCACAF region makes it hard for the US *not* to qualify for the finals. This time around, the team lost four games – one in the first group phase away to Costa Rica; then away to Mexico, at home to Honduras and away to the Costa Ricans again in the final phase.

Yet it was still enough for a third-place finish in the final group, on the same points tally as the second-placed Mexicans and three points clear of Honduras. One reason for the mixed form, American fans will point out, is that the team's style is more adventurous than it was, with less emphasis on keeping a clean sheet and more freedom given to the forwards, among whom Dutch-based **Earnie Stewart** top-scored with eight goals.

THE KEY PLAYER The son of an Argentine professional foot-baller and the man who, injuries permitting, will captain his country at this World Cup, **Claudio Reyna** may yet become the first soccer player to achieve genuine superstar status in America. Already a notable cult figure with his own range of branded sportswear and a celebrity wife – Danielle – who plays football for the US women's team, Reyna has achieved his fame despite spending the last eight years of his club career in Europe.

Reyna's skills have been honed in Germany and Britain

Reyna joined German club Bayer Leverkusen in 1994 and has since acted as a creative force in midfield for VfL Wolfsburg, Glasgow Rangers and Premiership club Sunderland. Though he has sometimes found goals hard to come by, his most valuable quality is his ability to lead a team – in terms of both tactics and morale.

THE EMERGING TALENT American teams – and their defences in particular – have often been criticised for their lack of pace. **DaMarcus Beasley** is an exception. Although he will only turn 20 just before the World Cup, the Chicago Fire full-back is hopeful of making the trip to Japan/Korea after being given his international debut in 2001. A series of tenacious displays during the USA's Gold Cup campaign added weight to his cause.

THE DUGOUT A former US international goalkeeper who coached the Under-23 team at the 1996 Atlanta Olympics and masterminded DC United's victory in the first-ever MLS Cup, **Bruce Arena** boasts as good a track record as any American-born soccer coach. While his Olympic experience stands him in good stead with the professionals who have since gone to Europe to improve their skills and bank balances, Arena's awareness of the MLS also leaves him well-placed to judge the next generation.

Since accepting his post in the aftermath of France '98, Arena has given 25 players their international debuts and invited almost 100 to training camps of various kinds. The result is that while the US may still lack star quality in some departments, strength in-depth is longer a problem.

CAMEROON
As they approach their fourth successive World Cup on the back of a second consecutive African Nations Cup triumph, it is hard to argue against Cameroon being the most successful of Africa's five representatives in Japan/Korea. The squad which came close to muscling its way into the second round at France '98 has been augmented with fresh blood from Cameroon's Under-23 side, which won Olympic football gold in Sydney two years ago. Only the habitual changes of coaching staff which seem to afflict this part of the football world threaten to spoil the picture – and the players have already proved themselves capable of living with that kind of turmoil.

THE PEDIGREE
Long before he was dancing his victory jig around the corner flags of Italia '90, Cameroon striker Roger Milla was giving us an equally memorable World Cup image – roaring in fury as he was given offside while racing away unchallenged against Italy at the 1982 tournament in **Spain**. As a result of that erroneous decision, Cameroon were held to a draw by the competition's eventual winners and failed to qualify for the second stage. Milla, a veteran even then, looked as though his moment of glory had passed him by.

Eight years later, the big man's recall to the Cameroon squad at the age of 38 smacked of desperation. Yet it was Milla's goals against Romania and Colombia, after François Omam-Biyik had given the team a shock win over Argentina in the tournament's opener, that took Cameroon into the quarter-finals of **Italia '90** – uncharted territory for any African side. Even then, it took two Gary Lineker penalties to deprive the 'Indomitable Lions' of further progress.

Four years on, with Milla again recalled at the age of 42, it was a different story. A side visibly lacking in motivation was no match for Brazil and Russia in the first phase, and left the **USA '94** party early. There was a similarly premature exit from **France '98**, but not before a younger, more robust team had held Austria to a 1–1 draw and then frustrated Chile by the same scoreline, despite being reduced to nine men.

THE ROAD TO JAPAN/KOREA
The Cameroonians played both legs of their first-round qualifier against Somalia at home for logistical reasons, and won both 3–0. That was the easy part; securing top spot in a second-round group containing emerging African teams such as Togo,

Zambia and Angola would be trickier. But superior experience, not to mention physical presence, counted heavily in Cameroon's favour. With goalkeeper **Alioum Boukar** and stoppers **Rigobert Song** and **Raymond Kalla** presenting a formidable obstacle, the team conceded only four goals in eight games – one fewer than striker **Patrick Mboma** (see below) scored as an individual.

THE KEY PLAYER
African footballer of the year for 2000 and, despite missing the final itself through injury, Cameroon's most dangerous player in their African Nations Cup triumph, **Patrick Mboma** couldn't be approaching this World Cup at a better time.

Now 31, Mboma was a late developer who spent years as understudy to George Weah at Paris Saint-Germain in the early 1990s. His only exposure to first-team football was at the tiny French club Châteauroux, to whom PSG loaned him for a year. In 1997 Mboma left France for the J-League club Gamba Osaka, for whom he averaged almost a goal a game. Subsequent career moves have taken him back to Europe with Italian clubs Cagliari and Parma, where goals have been harder to come by.

Mboma's goals brought glory in the African Nations Cup

THE EMERGING TALENT
An unlikely hero of Cameroon's African Nations Cup win, forward **Patrick Suffo** plays his club football in the English first division with Sheffield United. He arrived in South Yorkshire in the summer of 2000 but his debut was delayed after he served out a world-wide ban for spitting during a match for his previous club, Nantes. Now Suffo is making up for lost time with and has forged himself a regular first-team place for both club and country.

THE DUGOUT
Former Karlsruhe coach **Winfried Schäfer** did his chances of surviving until the World Cup the power of good when Cameroon beat Senegal on penalties to lift the African Nations Cup in February. His remains a controversial appointment, however, after the sacking of the popular Frenchman Pierre Lechantre.

GERMANY

GERMANY From victory over England at Wembley to humiliation by the same opponents in Munich, from the pain of losing 3–0 to the USA to the joy of qualifying for the World Cup with a 4–1 romp over Ukraine, these have been as bewildering a last couple of years as the German game can recall. The normally systematic and well-ordered progress of the national team has been rocked by a series of unforeseen setbacks, yet it says much about Germany's powers of resilience that the side, though a long way from being the best the country has produced, approaches this World Cup in both good form and good spirits.

THE PEDIGREE

THE PEDIGREE The Germans made no real impact on the World Cup until after World War II, when the nation was divided politically into East and West. Indeed, the country's lack of footballing pedigree was so great that West Germany were rank outsiders to win the trophy in **Switzerland** in 1954. Yet in the final German fitness and discipline were enough to outdo Hungarian guile, and a late Helmut Rahn goal won the match for the underdogs, 3–2.

West Germany's second final, in **England** in '66, would see the pendulum of fortune swing against them. But the game was also notable for the appearance of a young Franz Beckenbauer – a player who, eight years later in Munich, would lead out a more sophisticated German side for the 1974 final against their co-proponents of 'Total Football', Holland. Like the Hungarians two decades earlier, the Dutch went ahead quickly. But a controversial penalty and a piece of classic penalty-box opportunism from Gerd Müller then gave the hosts a lead they would not relinquish.

If there was a suspicion that the best team had lost the '74 final, there was no doubt the better side won the last game of **Italia '90**, a late penalty beating Argentina – giving Beckenbauer, now the coach, a unique World Cup double, and the country revenge for a 3–2 defeat four years earlier.

Despite the reunification of East and West Germany which followed, there has been no hint of a fourth World Cup. A 2–1 defeat by Bulgaria in the quarter-finals of **USA '94** was a shock; a 3–0 mauling by Croatia at the same stage four years ago was nothing less than a humiliation.

THE ROAD TO JAPAN/KOREA

THE ROAD TO JAPAN/KOREA When **Dietmar Hamann**'s long-range effort skidded across the Wembley turf to give Germany a 1–0 win over England in October 2000, his team's path to the finals seemed clear. Yet within less than a year, England had created five chances in the return in Munich, taken all five of them, and left the Germans heading for the play-offs.

Fortunately, Germany's legendary powers of recovery quickly kicked into action. A 5–2 aggregate win over Ukraine, inspired by a driven **Michael Ballack** and aided by some vital saves from intimidating 'keeper **Oliver Kahn**, was enough to write out a replacement World Cup ticket for the one Michael Owen's hat-trick had snatched away.

THE KEY PLAYER There are always a handful of players for whom the World Cup arrives at just the right time, and **Michael Ballack** might just be one of them. The Bayer Leverkusen midfielder is in a rich vein of scoring form for both club and country (he scored six in Germany's qualifying campaign) but, more importantly, his intelligent use of the ball and range of passing look capable of giving the Germans a flexibility they have lacked since the tragically early retirement of Matthias Sammer.

Such is Ballack's elegance on the ball that he has even been compared with Beckenbauer, prompting the nickname 'Little Kaiser'. That may prove a heavy burden for the 25-year-old to bear, but if he can handle the hype, Ballack will have a World Cup to savour.

THE EMERGING TALENT If Ballack provides the poise, then **Sebastian Deisler** offers the youthful energy missing from Germany's lumbering class of '98. Constantly on the move and hard for defenders to pin down, the 22-year-old Hertha Berlin forward has been his country's 'great white hope' more or less ever since he made his *Bundesliga* debut in 1999. The only question mark, aside from Deisler's inexperience, hangs over his fragility – a knee injury sustained last October was the latest in a series of knocks to have required surgery.

THE DUGOUT Having been offered the post as caretaker after Euro 2000, **Rudi Völler** became coach on a permanent basis once the man originally intended to take over in 2001, Christoph Daum, became embroiled in a drugs scandal. Interestingly, there were no 'turnip' cartoons after Völler's side had crashed 5–1 to England, the German media instead offering sympathy to the former international striker who had inherited such a mess. Will Völler need more of the same after the World Cup?

IRELAND

After play-off defeats in the run-up to the last three major international tournaments, the Irish made it fourth time lucky for Japan/Korea and, many would argue, deservedly so. Big Jack's boys in green may have given the world a fright with their gung-ho approach in the late 1980s and early '90s, but the next generation, while treating its inheritance with due respect, has also given it a new dimension. Mick McCarthy's Ireland are young, smart and deftly confident. Just by way of a change, a large number of them were also actually born in the Republic.

THE PEDIGREE

Ireland had never made it to the final stages of any tournament prior to their appearance at Euro '88 in West Germany, and two years later they arrived at **Italia '90** as World Cup novices. Yet Jack Charlton's squad was nothing if not disciplined and tenacious – they drew all three of their group games, winning second place behind England thanks to the spin of a coin. In the second round they ground out a goal-less draw with Romania and kept their nerve to win the shoot-out, and while their ultimate 1–0 defeat by Italy in Rome was more one-sided than the scoreline suggested, the Irish had undoubtedly made their mark.

For all their progress, Jack's men had not won a World Cup match in open play. That was to change at **USA '94**, when Ray Houghton's long-range shot gave them a revenge victory over Italy in New York. Defeat by Mexico and a stalemate with Norway were just enough to see the Irish through to the second round again, but in the same midday Florida heat which had stifled them against the Mexicans, Ireland wilted against Holland, losing 2–0.

THE ROAD TO JAPAN/KOREA

After Holland (Euro '96), Belgium (France '98) and Turkey (Euro 2000) had all put paid to Irish ambitions in recent play-offs, few supporters relished the prospect of the two-leg tie against Iran which stood between them and a place at this World Cup. But a comfortable 2–0 win in Dublin laid the foundation for a solid defensive performance in the second leg in Tehran, the Iranians only grabbing a goal back when it was too late.

The real achievement, though, lay in winning a play-off berth in the first place. Drawn in Europe's 'group of death' alongside Holland and Portugal, Ireland were widely expected to struggle. In the event they went all ten games unbeaten, holding the Portuguese to two draws, going two up against the Dutch in Amsterdam before being pegged back to 2–2 late on, then beating the same opposition in Dublin with a **Jason McAteer** goal, despite being reduced to ten men for the last half-hour.

Roy Keane leads by example as Ireland's workaholic captain

THE KEY PLAYER A vital part of Ireland's midfield jigsaw since USA '94, **Roy Keane** now has another chance to prove his mettle on the international stage. The success of Manchester United has meant the former amateur boxer has rarely been out of the limelight since that last World Cup appearance. But whereas at Old Trafford Keane is merely one star in a galaxy of many, in the Irish setup he is obliged to lead a squad of younger, less certain talents by example. That has inevitably meant toning down some of the aggression which once characterised Keane's attitude to the game, particularly since the Charlton regime gave way to McCarthy's more considered approach. Yet his ability to 'mix it' when necessary, to cover every blade of grass and to dictate the play by making every touch count remains undiminished.

THE EMERGING TALENT Scoring goals from anything other than a big punt upfield or a well-rehearsed set piece once seemed anathema to the Irish, but a new wave of attack-minded players is changing all that. Typical of the breed is **Robbie Keane**, who at the age of 21 already has eight international goals to his name.

Quick-witted as well as quick-footed, Keane can play in wide or withdrawn roles as well as in the classic centre-forward position, and survived a bizarre nine-month spell with Inter Milan to cement his standing – both in the national side and at club level with Leeds United.

THE DUGOUT Having initially struggled to shake off the shadow of his mentor Jack Charlton, **Mick McCarthy** has matured into a national coach of real stature. His knowledge of the Irish setup has poved more important than generic coaching experience, and his faith in Ireland's players – not to mention the FAI's faith in him – finally got its just rewards in Tehran last November.

SAUDI ARABIA

There are two distinct sides to the Saudi footballing character, and few indications as to which will be on show in Japan/Korea. Will it be the face of style and enterprise which captivated neutrals at USA '94? Or that of safety first and gamesmanship – the traits which so disfigured the nation's campaign in France four years later? Much will depend on the choice of players and tactics, but even here, predictions are made difficult by the tendency of the Saudi princes who run the game in this oil-rich Gulf state to chop and change coaches from one month to the next.

THE PEDIGREE

Despite an impressive record in Asian tournaments, the Saudis arrived unheralded at **USA '94** – dismissed as a team of spoilt brats whose lack of fitness and incentives would undermine their undoubted potential. The cynics were proved wrong within 20 minutes of the Saudis' opening game, when they took the lead against Holland. The match was lost, but wins over Morocco and Belgium (the latter featuring the goal of the tournament from Saeed al-Owairan) then followed, and the Arabs' enterprising and athletic style troubled Sweden for much of the second-round tie between the two – despite a final 3–1 scoreline in the Scandinavians' favour.

At **France '98** it was a different story. The tournament's referees were grappling with Sepp Blatter's unworkable tackle-from-behind ruling, and the Saudis were unlucky to be a man down after just 19 minutes against the hosts. But they had already lost their opening game 1–0 to Denmark, and defeat by France rendered irrelevant their final 2–2 draw against South Africa, a game scarred by Saudi gamesmanship which 'earned' them two doubtful penalties – incidents which would test another new FIFA rule if repeated in Japan/Korea.

THE ROAD TO JAPAN/KOREA

After sailing untroubled through a first-round group containing such giants of the global game as Vietnam, Bangladesh and Mongolia, the Saudis hit choppier seas in the second of Asia's two qualifying phases. Hard-fought draws at home to Bahrain and Iran, coupled with defeat away to the latter, left them needing to win their last game at home to Thailand and hope that the Iranians would lose in Bahrain. That was exactly how it turned out, Iran flunking their big moment by losing 3–1 and Saudi Arabia beating the Thais 4–1.

THE KEY PLAYER He will not turn 30 until after the World Cup, yet striker **Sami al-Jaber** has already enjoyed 12 years of international football with his country. A veteran of both the USA '94 and France '98 campaigns, he scored in both – becoming the first Asian player to find the net in consecutive World Cups.

Comfortable in the role of either target-man or deep-lying forward, al-Jaber has spent most of his club career in Saudi Arabia, having returned disillusioned from a loan spell in the English first division with Wolves two years ago.

THE EMERGING TALENT The critics who upbraided Saudi Arabia for their lacklustre displays in qualifying chose to overlook the fact that the team's brightest young hope, **Nawaf al-Temyat**, had to sit out the whole process with knee ligament damage.

A 25-year-old team-mate of al-Jaber at the al-Hilal club, al-Temyat provides the through balls for the more experienced man to latch onto, while his acceleration in the middle of the park is a welcome shot in the arm to a Saudi team that can sometimes look once-paced.

Al-Temyat's return gives the Saudis much-needed new options

Prior to his injury – from which he has now recovered – al-Temyat was named Asian footballer of the year for 2000.

THE DUGOUT Appointed coach in October 2000, then again some 13 months later, Saudi-born **Nasser al-Johar** appears to have the confidence of the princes who pay his salary – at least for now. He replaced Milan Machala prior to the start of the Asian qualifying phase, then promptly lost his job to Slobodan Santrac before the second round, the princes apparently reasoning that a foreign manager was needed as Saudi Arabia's opposition got tougher. Defeat by Bahrain soon disabused them of that notion, and al-Johar returned to see the Saudis home. He is assisted by an entourage of consultants, mostly from Brazil and former Yugoslavia.

ARGENTINA
Winners of two World Cups, Argentina approach this year's tournament with arguably their strongest-ever squad, widely tipped to capture a third. All the ingredients for success appear to be in place, not least a string of highly rated, European-based players to whom indiscipline – so often the nation's Achilles heel in the past – no longer comes as second nature. The only worry is that the pressure from back home, where their country stands on the brink of political and economic collapse, will be so intense that Argentina may wilt under it.

THE PEDIGREE
Argentina contested the first-ever World Cup final, in **Uruguay** in 1930, but after taking a 2–1 lead at one stage were beaten 4–2 by their hosts. It was to be decades before the nation qualified for the finals again, and when they did reach **England** in 1966, they lost a glorified brawl of a quarter-final 1–0 to the eventual winners.

On home soil in 1978, it would be a very different story. Argentina were not the best team in the tournament, but theirs was the most compact unit, driven by the combination of coach César Luis Menotti and captain Daniel Passarella, and inspired by the midfield flair of the diminutive Osvaldo Ardiles. After a treading a controversial path, they beat Holland 3–1 in the final in Buenos Aires, becoming national heroes overnight.

Argentina relinquished their trophy in **Spain** in 1982, but not before they had introduced the world to Diego Maradona, a stocky forward with a fiery temper who some were touting as the best footballer in the world. In **Mexico** four years later, Maradona justified the hype, scoring majestic solo goals against England and Belgium before taking a back seat in a memorable, two-goals-in-the-last-three-minutes final against West Germany, which his team won 3–2.

The Germans gained their revenge at **Italia '90**, in an infinitely less memorable final. Here and in the States four years later, the world would see a more cynical Argentina and an increasingly tragi-comic Maradona – his tortured knees now good only for hoodwinking referees, his athleticism sustained (as it turned out) by a cocktail of illegal drugs.

Yet at **France '98** the Argentines had re-invented themselves again. Now with Passarella as coach, they played some of the tournament's most beguiling football, beat England on penalties after an epic second-round tie, and were then unlucky to lose to an even more inspired Holland in the quarter-finals.

THE ROAD TO JAPAN/KOREA One reason for Argentina being so strongly fancied is the manner in which they qualified for the finals. From the moment **Gabriel Batistuta** had set them on the way to a 4–1 trouncing of Chile ten minutes into the campaign, the Argentines imposed themselves on the South American pool in a way no other team has managed. Their only defeat in 18 games was away to Brazil, and after that only three further points were dropped. Most impressive was the team's relentless attacking. Not once in the campaign did Argentina fail to score, with Batistuta, **Claudio López**, **Hernán Crespo** and **Ariel Ortega** all contributing to a goal tally of 42.

THE KEY PLAYER It says much about **Gabriel Batistuta** that at 33 years of age, and despite the surfeit of other goalscoring options in Argentina's ranks, it is unthinkable that he would be left out of the squad for Japan/Korea. The crude statistics (five goals in qualifying, 20 in Roma's *scudetto*-winning season of 2000/01) are still impressive, but arguably more important is the presence of *BatiGol* as a talismanic figure.

If age has not dimmed his goalscoring instincts, it has matured him into a genuine leader of men. This may be Batistuta's last World Cup, but if it goes according to form, it is unlikely to be his quietest.

THE EMERGING TALENT Just as Spain '82 came a little too early for a young Maradona, so this year's contest may be a World Cup too soon for **Pablo Aimar**. The slightly built 22-year-old is the latest in a long line of ingenious Argentine midfielders, but has suffered from a lack of first-team football since moving to Spanish club Valéncia in January 2001. Even so, he is likely to be picked for the squad, if only to gain vital experience for greater challenges ahead.

THE DUGOUT When Daniel Passarella quit after France '98, it seemed Argentina had lost the architect most capable of building another World Cup-winning side. Yet **Marcelo Bielsa** has proved a worthy replacement, shedding some of the disciplinarian excesses of his predecessor and getting more spontaneity from his players as payback. Bielsa's unusual twist on the sweeper system, in which a second row of three players sits in front of the defence, looks negative on paper but, in reality, has provided the perfect springboard for his team's progressive instincts.

ENGLAND
From the depths of despair which accompanied home defeat by Germany and Kevin Keegan's resignation at the start of the qualifiers, England now exude a confidence which, at international level, can only be brought about by coaching of the highest standard. With relatively few changes to either personnel or tactics, Sven Göran Eriksson has injected a fresh sense of purpose into the squad through the medium of his own self-belief. The result is that while England may not win this World Cup, they will go into it better-prepared than for any major tournament since 1966.

THE PEDIGREE
England may have been the birthplace of the modern game, but the FA were initially sceptical about the idea of a World Cup, dismissing it as an expensive novelty. As a consequence, the English did not participate at all until 1950, when a formidable line-up including Alf Ramsey, Billy Wright, Stan Mortensen and Tom Finney travelled to **Brazil** as one of the favourites. In a classic tale of under-preparation, they were beaten 1–0 by the USA and did not progress beyond the group stage.

Things gradually improved through the next three World Cups, but it wasn't until the appointment of Alf Ramsey as manager before the 1966 finals – which England would host – that a team of real purpose was created. Ramsey's emphasis on discipline and work-rate went down like a lead balloon with the romantics. But his 'wingless wonders', playing all their games at Wembley, were unstoppable, and Geoff Hurst became the first (and so far only) man to score a hat-trick in a World Cup final as West Germany were beaten 4–2 after extra time. The Germans gained their revenge in **Mexico** four years later, when an arguably better England side were two-up and coasting in their quarter-final but contrived to lose 3–2.

The remainder of the 1970s were wilderness years for England, and while **Spain '82** and **Mexico '86** both saw spirited displays (curtailed by Keegan's injury and Maradona's Hand of God, respectively), it wasn't until Italia '90 that England made a credible challenge for the World Cup. Bobby Robson's team saved their best football of the tournament for the semi-final against West Germany, but lost on penalties.

Graham Taylor succeeded Robson and failed to get England to **USA '94**, but Glenn Hoddle's side would surely have gone further had they not come up against Argentina – and the inevitable shoot-out defeat – in the second round of France '98.

THE ROAD TO JAPAN/KOREA

England's opening defeat by Germany and the subsequent resignation of manager Keegan couldn't have made for a less promising start. A goalless draw in Finland then made matters worse. But once Eriksson had joined the setup in the spring of 2001, England's football – and results – measurably improved.

While the coach's influence cannot be over-stated, another factor in the turnaround was the enforced departure from Wembley. Anfield, St James' Park and Old Trafford all roared their encouragement as England beat Finland and Albania and, in the dying seconds, got the draw they needed against Greece thanks to **David Beckham**'s immortal free-kick.

THE KEY PLAYER

England's 5–1 romp over Germany confirmed **Michael Owen**'s elevation to the status of an international-class striker. Plagued by injuries since scoring his wonder-goal as an 18-year-old against Argentina in '98, then often misused by Keegan when he was fit, Owen proved in Munich that if the ball is played as he likes it – deep, early and in front of him – there is no better player in Europe at taking on the last man and finishing from distance.

The bad news for England fans is that Owen's game will always make him more injury-prone than, say, a classic target-man in the Alan Shearer mould. The good news is that, even after Japan/Korea, if he stays fit he could star in another three World Cups.

THE EMERGING TALENT

Though he has not played for England since the disastrous home defeat by Germany, **Kieron Dyer** remains one of the country's most intriguing prospects. The 23-year-old Newcastle forward is quick, reliable and versatile but, most importantly in England terms, he is naturally left-sided.

A foot injury ruled him out for the early part of 2002 but, as his club manager Bobby Robson says, Dyer's return will be worth the wait.

THE DUGOUT

The cynics who branded the appointment of Swedish-born **Sven Göran Eriksson** as treachery 18 months ago were soon forced to eat their words. The genial former Gothenburg, Benfica and Lazio coach has impressed the nation with his quiet thoroughness and, perhaps more importantly in the shadow of the Hoddle and Keegan eras, seems to have the implicit trust of his players.

NIGERIA

The most successful African nation of the 1990s has also been the region's most consistent producer of fresh talent. But there are signs that, just as the World Cup beckons, the production line of young Nigerian stars is stuttering to a halt, leaving an ageing team searching for inspiration if it is to build on earlier achievements. They will still be great to watch, but there will be no room for complacency.

THE PEDIGREE

The Nigerians did not make their World Cup debut until **USA '94** – but it was worth waiting for. Already crowned as African champions that year, a team driven forward by the prolific strike-force of Daniel Amokachi and Rashidi Yekini crushed Bulgaria and Greece in the opening group phase, then came within three minutes of knocking out Italy and earning a place in the quarter-finals.

At **France '98**, a less spontaneous but still potent squad, bristling with confidence after winning football gold at the 1996 Atlanta Olympics, came from behind twice to beat Spain in their opening game, then edged Bulgaria 1–0 to book their second-round place a match early. But a much-changed if not quite 'reserve' team then lost Nigeria's last group match to Paraguay, and precious momentum had been lost. The sense of anti-climax was palpable as Denmark put four past the Nigerians in their second-round tie at the Stade de France. The so-called 'Super Eagles' had been brought crashing down to Earth.

Agali's goals rescued Nigeria during the qualifying phase

THE ROAD TO JAPAN/KOREA

The Nigerians recovered from being held to a goalless draw in Eritrea to beat the same opposition 4–0 at home, thereby qualifying for Africa's second-round group stage. There the competition was somewhat stiffer – including an improving Sudan side as well as the established African powers of Ghana and Liberia.

A couple of away defeats – to Liberia and, more surprisingly, Sierra Leone – almost put a spanner in the works, but a timely return to form and fitness by **Kanu** and the goals of emerging striker **Victor Agali** (see below) got the team back on track, and as their rivals contrived to take points off each other, a 3–0 home win over Ghana saw Nigeria through.

THE KEY PLAYER On the periphery of the action in 1994, a pivotal figure in France four years later, **Jay-Jay Okocha** approaches his third World Cup with a few points still to prove.

At club level, the £10million transfer from Turkey to France which made him the most expensive African player of all time has turned out to be insufficient to turn Paris Saint-Germain into continent-beaters – and Okocha is rumoured to be looking for a move to the English Premiership for 2002/03. Internationally, while his extravagant ball skills continue to delight neutrals, Nigeria's fans want him to mature and become more of a team player – an increasingly important role now that he is a senior member of the squad. Whether Okocha can complete that process in time for Japan/Korea, and without compromising his unique individual talents, remains to be seen.

THE EMERGING TALENT The Nigerians turn over front players with alarming speed. Fortunately, there always seems to be another youngster waiting in the wings the moment an established star burns out. **Victor Agali** is the latest of the young bloods, a 23-year-old goal-poacher who was discovered by Olympique Marseille in 1996.

Agali has been in Europe ever since, his talents being honed and ruggedised in the uncompromising atmosphere of Hansa Rostock for three seasons, before a move to Schalke coincided with his best run in the Nigerian national side in 2001.

THE DUGOUT Nigeria went into the last two World Cups with foreign management teams, and it remains to be seen whether **Amodu Shaibu**, one of the few indigenous coaches to occupy the top job, can fight retain his post for Japan/Korea. Though praised for encouraging young talents at a time when Nigeria needs them more than ever, his tolerance of the casual attitude exhibited by some of the older players was criticised after Nigeria's African Nations Cup semi-final defeat by Senegal.

SWEDEN

A nation whose footballing fortunes have fluctuated wildly through the 1990s, Sweden now seeks an era of stability to help rebuild its domestic game, which is shedding young talent with a speed that makes every earlier exodus seem paltry by comparison. The Swedes qualified impressively for Euro 2000 but seemed bewildered at the finals themselves. The task facing the coaching duo of Tommy Söderberg and Lars Lagerbäck is to ensure there is no repeat performance in Japan/Korea.

THE PEDIGREE

Like the rest of their fellow Scandinavians, the Swedes were enthusiastic amateurs whose purist approach to football left them ill-prepared for developing tournaments such as the World Cup. Being the host nation in 1958 gave the national side an advantage it exploited to the full, the once-banned professionals who had taken Sweden to Olympic football gold ten years earlier being welcomed back to the fold just in time. Stirring wins over the Soviet Union and West Germany earned a rendezvous with Brazil in the final, where the ageing hosts were no match for their younger, more spontaneous guests, and were thrashed 5–2.

After that Swedish club football began to assert itself on the European stage, but the 1960s, '70s and '80s were barren times for the national side. A much-hyped team travelled to **Italia '90** under Olle Nordin and contrived to lose all three of their games, and even while hosting the European Championship two years later, the Swedes were overshadowed by their neighbours, Denmark.

The core of the Euro '92 side held promise, though, and inspired by three all-time greats (goalkeeper Thomas Ravelli, playmaker Tomas Brolin and target man Kennet Andersson), Sweden made it all the way to the semi-finals of **USA '94**, losing narrowly to Brazil before mauling Bulgaria in the play-off to take third place – the country's best World Cup finish yet.

THE ROAD TO JAPAN/KOREA

The Swedes needed an easy group to help them get over the disappointments of Euro 2000, and by and large they got it. Slovakia, Macedonia and Moldova were no match for the men in yellow, and not even Turkey, a nation that has given Sweden problems in the past, could stand in the way once Henrik Larsson and Andreas Andersson had grabbed two goals in the last three minutes to overturn a 1–0 deficit in Istanbul.

THE KEY PLAYER Too young to be considered for USA '94, too burdened by a slow-to-heal calf injury to make an impact at Euro 2000, **Henrik Larsson** now has a glorious opportunity to show the world what he can do.

The 30-year-old forward, whose prolific goalscoring helped shift the balance of power in Scottish domestic football after his move from Feyenoord to Celtic in 1997, is the antithesis of the archetypal Scandinavian striker: slightly built, quick off the mark and better on the edge of the box than on the six-yard line.

With his country as with his club, Larsson benefits from having his team-mates play around him – he is the undisputed star of both. Yet, for a player whose quick reactions are such an essential part of his game, Japan/Korea may be his last chance to truly shine on the biggest stage of all.

Larsson needs to prove he can compete at the highest level

THE EMERGING TALENT Disciplined, enthusiastic, increasingly tactically aware and keen to increase their earning potential, Swedish players are natural targets for foreign clubs – and the Premiership especially. One of the latest Swedes to make an impact in England is Southampton midfielder **Anders Svensson**.

Bought by former Saints manager Stuart Gray as a wide player, Svensson was moved infield by Gordon Strachan, a role closer to the one he performs for the national team. Like many Swedes he initially struggled to cope with the increased pace and physicality of Premiership football, but now feels quite at home – and how ironic it would be if his acclimatisation to the English way helped him defeat England themselves in Japan/Korea.

THE DUGOUT Sweden's unique coaching duo of **Tommy Söderberg** and **Lars Lagerbäck** tend to look uncharacteristically relaxed for national-team bosses. Their secret, perhaps, lies in the division of duties which ensures neither is overworked. As Söderberg himself puts it: "Lars is the tactical genius; I'm the players' man."

CROATIA

Everyone's favourite underdogs at France '98, the Croats have proved their ability to regenerate by shedding their seemingly irreplaceable coach, waving goodbye to some veteran players, yet still qualifying for Japan/Korea without losing a match. The likely squad still looks a little on the old side but, with an unbeaten record against their main group rivals Italy, Croatia may feel confident of progress once again.

THE PEDIGREE

Croat players were often among the most creative in Yugoslav national sides, and indeed the core of Yugoslavia's 1987 World Youth Cup-winning squad was Croatian. Contemporary Croat stars among those youthful champions included Robert Prosinecki, who played for Yugoslavia at **Italia '90**, and Davor Suker, who made the squad but saw no first-team action.

> Prosinecki is a survivor from Yugoslavia's Italia '90 squad

After achieving independence from Yugoslavia, Croatia qualified for Euro '96, the first major tournament they were permitted to enter. At the finals in England, Suker's showmanship led the Croats as far as a quarter-final with Germany at Old Trafford – an ill-tempered tie which Croatia were unlucky to lose 2–1.

Suker was back among the goals at **France '98**. The former Real Madrid striker's Golden Boot-winning haul of six included the twice-taken penalty that beat Romania in the second round; the second of three in the quarter-finals as the Croats gained revenge over the Germans; and the opener in a 2–1 defeat by France in the semi-finals. Just for good measure, Suker added another in the third-place play-of against Holland, which Croatia won to seal a remarkable World Cup debut.

THE ROAD TO JAPAN/KOREA

After being edged out of a place at Euro 2000 by (of all people) Yugoslavia, the Croats turned over a new leaf for the World Cup qualifiers. Out went coach Ciro Blazevic and his trusted captain, Zvonimir Boban. In came Mirko Jozic and a number of new players including brothers **Niko** and **Robert Kovac, Bosko Balaban** and **Davor Vugrinec**. But if the names were different, the storyline they acted out was familiar. Croatia stuck to their quick counter-attacking game, a well-disciplined defence conceding just two goals in eight group matches.

And, as in the past, the Croats were masters at adapting their style to suit the opposition. **Prosinecki** and **Alen Boksic** went on goal sprees against the likes of Latvia and San Marino. But serious rivals Scotland and Belgium were handled with greater care; Boksic's goal 15 minutes from the end against the Belgians in Zagreb was sufficient for top spot.

THE KEY PLAYER The only member of Croatia's 'golden generation' to return to play his club football at home, **Robert Prosinecki** made yet another unexpected move in the summer of 2001, when he left Dinamo Zagreb for Portsmouth. Yet the transfer has breathed fresh life into the 33-year-old midfielder's career.

Noticeably fitter and with a healthier appetite for the game than he has displayed for some time, Prosinecki is nonetheless cautious about Croatia's prospects in what will surely be his last major tournament, openly criticising the nation's media for billing every game as 'historic'.

THE EMERGING TALENT With the mercurial Suker currently without a club, a legion of understudies is striving for consideration in Croatia's World Cup squad. Among the latest contenders is **Tomislav Maric**, a 29-year-old who has Croat nationality despite being born in Germany and having spent his entire professional career there.

Now at VfL Wolfsburg where he has been nicknamed *Mister Doppelpack* because of his knack for scoring two goals in a game, Maric remains relatively little-known in Croatia despite having played for the Under-21 side. Will it be a case of out-of-sight, out-of-mind?

THE DUGOUT The wind of political change blew through the Croatian FA when they appointed **Mirko Jozic** as national-team boss two years ago. Like many coaches from the former Yugoslavia, the 61-year-old had achieved most abroad – in Jozic's case with the Chilean club Colo Colo. His status as an 'outsider' made it easier for him to make a break with the previous Croat regime, and so far the results of his inventive and thorough approach have justified the faith of his FA bosses.

ECUADOR

Of all the stories surrounding this year's World Cup debutants, Ecuador's is the most romantic. No other newcomer had to play so many games to get this far, nor against so many rivals with more illustrious World Cup histories behind them. On the face of it, further progress – away from the hysterical crowds and high altitude of Ecuador's Andean base at Quito, which made such a contribution in qualifying – is unlikely. But the Ecuadoreans have already shown that they relish the role of underdog, and will be nobody's easy meat.

THE PEDIGREE

This tiny South American nation, which derives its name from the equator that runs through the middle of its territory, has no previous World Cup track-record. Indeed, it has no real footballing record at all, a fourth-place finish in 1993 being Ecuador's best performance in the Copa America.

Yet unlike Venezuela, the other nation which has tended to be landed with the wooden spoon whenever South America has engaged in international competition, Ecuador is not a country preoccupied with other sports such as baseball. Football is as vital to life here as it is in Brazil, Argentina or Uruguay, and at club level, the major Ecuadorean sides such as Barcelona Guayaquil and Emelec have enjoyed good runs in the Copa Libertadores, the former reaching the final in 1998.

THE ROAD TO JAPAN/KOREA

Like all other South American teams, Ecuador were obliged to play a minimum of 18 games in qualifying. They started slowly, but in October 2000 set off on a run of five straight wins – including a 1–0 victory over Brazil in Quito, courtesy of an **Augustín Delgado** goal – which was enough to hoist them into the mini-league's top four.

Once there, the Ecuadoreans never left the qualification zone. They shrugged off a defeat in Argentina; put five past hapless Bolivia in La Paz to prove they were more than just a team of home bankers; then secured their World Cup berth with one game to spare, drawing 1–1 at home to Uruguay, **Iván Kaviedes** finishing off a move involving Delgado and Alex Aguinaga to cancel out Nicolas Oliveira's first-half penalty.

THE KEY PLAYER

Joint top scorer in the South American qualifiers alongside Argentina's Hernán Crespo, **Augustín Delgado** is nothing less than a national hero in his native Ecuador. A veteran of the Barcelona Guayaquil side which became the first Ecuadorean club to reach the Copa Libertadores final in 1998, he began his career as a central defender – a role to which he attributes his outstanding aerial ability and threatening pace.

After Barcelona's Copa Libertadores run, *El Tín* moved to Cruz Azúl and then Necaxa of Mexico, appearing for the latter in FIFA's fledgling World Club Championship. At the end of 2001, Delgado and his fellow countryman Cleber Chalá were signed by Premiership club Southampton.

THE EMERGING TALENT

Though he only became a first-team regular during the qualifiers, striker **Iván Kaviedes** leads the Ecuadorean line with the nonchalance of a much more experienced player.

Unlike most of his countrymen, the lanky 24-year-old forward has learnt his trade in European football, and it has not been an altogether happy experience.

Kaviedes brings precious European experience to the side

Having left his homeland to join the Italian *Serie A* club Perugia in 1998, Kaviedes played just four games before being sold to Celta Vigo of Spain a year later. At Celta he fared even less well, struggling with his fitness and eventually being loaned out to Real Valladolid for the 2001/02 season. Now the 2002/03 campaign looks like seeing Kaviedes switching countries yet again, this time to join FC Porto. But in the meantime, he will have a much bigger stage on which to show his doubting club bosses what he is made of.

THE DUGOUT

A controversial appointment, Colombian-born **Hernán Dario Gomez** has often chosen publicly to play down Ecuador's chances of glory in the face of intense media hype. It was a tactic which worked in qualifying, but whether Gomez can keep his players' feet on the ground in the finals is another matter.

ITALY Having reached the final of Euro 2000 with what critics back home dismissed as a mediocre team, the *Azzurri* have every right to be confident now that their 'mediocrity' has had a further two years in which to mature. The resignation of coach Dino Zoff immediately after Italy's defeat by France two years ago was a shock to the system, yet the incumbent Giovanni Trapattoni did the right thing by sticking with the same group of players. The consequence is that the Italians approach this World Cup against a background of rare stability and consensus – and the rest had better watch out.

THE PEDIGREE One of the most enthusiastic of all European nations toward the fledgling World Cup, Italy won both the 1934 and '38 editions of the tournament – the first by beating Czechoslovakia 2–1 on home soil, the second with a 4–2 win over Hungary in **France**. Both teams were coached by Vittorio Pozzo, whose adoption of central European tactics was the catalyst for Italy's footballing development, but whose work was brought to an abrupt end by World War II.

For much of the 1950s and '60s, Italian football was disfigured by *catenaccio*, a rigidly defensive formation which dominated the domestic game, and by an influx of foreign imports to the *Serie A* which halted the progress of homegrown players. Things got so bad that foreign players were banned altogether in 1964, but that didn't prevent Italy's darkest World Cup hour – a 1–0 defeat by North Korea in **England** in '66, a result which prompted fans to hurl rotten tomatoes at the Italian squad as they returned home.

A new generation of players did emerge, however, to take Italy to the European Championship in 1968 and the World Cup final in **Mexico** four years later, where the *Azzurri* were outplayed by Brazil, 4–1. They returned to South America eight years later to earn a fourth-place finish in **Argentina**, and the core of that team, cannily coached by Enzo Bearzot and pushed from the back by goalkeeper-captain Dino Zoff, beat West Germany 3–1 for Italy's third World Cup win in **Spain** in 1982.

Since then the Italians have hinted at further glory but never quite attained it. After losing their crown in **Mexico** in 1986, they departed from three successive tournaments on penalties – against Argentina in 1990, Brazil in the final of USA '94, and the eventual winners **France** four years ago.

THE ROAD TO JAPAN/KOREA Rebounding quickly from the disappointment of losing the Euro 2000 final, the Italians were scarcely troubled by their qualifying section. A 2–2 draw with Hungary in Budapest looked as though it might signal a rockier road but, remarkably, a defence marshalled as ever by the evergreen **Paolo Maldini** conceded only one further goal in seven games.

With **Alessandro del Piero**, **Francesco Totti**, **Pippo Inzaghi** and **Marco Delvecchio** all finding their goalscoring form, Italy brushed past Romania, Lithuania and Georgia, sealing top spot in the group with a game to spare.

THE KEY PLAYER If it falls to a single player to inspire Italy to victory in this World Cup, then coach Trapattoni believes that man will be **Francesco Totti**. Having made his international debut just after France '98, the Roma forward will be tasting the unique atmosphere of the competition for the first time. Yet there is nothing to suggest he will be overawed by the occasion.

The 25-year-old was outstanding both at Euro 2000 and in Italy's World Cup qualifying campaign, his vision giving the *Azzurri* fresh options going forward, his commitment proving infectious among his team-mates. For Roma, too, he has been irrepressible, providing a key component in the 2000/01 title-winning side, and this year signing a new contract which will keep him at the club he supported as a boy until 2005.

THE EMERGING TALENT Less likely to make headlines than a Totti or a del Piero, but a vital player nonetheless, **Gianluca Zambrotta** is the latest in a long line of reliable Italian midfield anchormen. Having moved from Bari to Juventus for £10million in 1999, he forced his way into Italy's Euro 2000 squad and has been a rock for both club and country ever since.

THE DUGOUT Filling the shoes of the popular Dino Zoff was never going to be easy, but **Giovanni Trapattoni** has gone about his work with the minimum of fuss – as befits one of the most successful coaches in European football history. Even discounting his achievements as a player for AC Milan, *Trap* can still boast seven league titles and five European trophy wins. The World Cup would be the icing on a very grand cake.

MEXICO

The Mexicans are the great under-achievers of world football. In this part of the world the game is a religion in all but name and, as Robert Prosinecki has pointed out, there are more registered players in Mexico than there are *people* in Croatia. Yet despite hosting the World Cup twice and producing scores of world-class players, the Mexicans have never come close to winning soccer's ultimate accolade. This year, as ever, a talented but unpredictable squad will do well to come through the group stage.

THE PEDIGREE

With their mighty superpower neighbour slow to get bitten by the football bug, Mexico usually qualified for the finals without too much trouble – even when their CONCACAF region had only one place available to it. The upshot is that 2002 will see the Mexicans appearing in their 13th World Cup and, with CONCACAF members now entitled to three berths, there look certain to be many more.

Qualifying for the finals and making a big impact on them are two very different things, however. It wasn't until Mexico hosted the tournament for the first time, in 1970, that the team made its mark. After a dour goalless draw in the inaugural game against the Soviet Union, the Mexicans beat El Salvador and Belgium – still without conceding a goal. They finished on the same goal difference as the Soviets, and were given top spot in the group by the drawing of lots. A fat lot of good it did them – they were thrashed 4–1 by Italy in the quarter-finals.

Sixteen years later, after **Mexico** had stepped in to host the tournament following Colombia's withdrawal, a more ambitious side led by legendary striker Hugo Sánchez cruised through an easy first-round group, then beat a tired Bulgaria in the second round. They then took West Germany all the way in a fiercely contested quarter-final in Monterrey, but were beaten 4–1 on penalties.

THE ROAD TO JAPAN/KOREA

The Mexicans played their way through two group phases on the way to the finals, and did not look convincing in either of them. An early defeat away to Trinidad & Tobago meant having to settle for second place in the first round, while a home loss to Costa Rica (the first-ever for Mexico's full national side in the Azteca stadium) resulted in the depature of coach Enrique Meza midway through the second stage. The appointment of Javier Aguirre as Meza's replacement also heralded the welcome return of influential midfielder **Alberto García Aspe**, and with striker **Cuauhtémoc Blanco** rediscovering his form, Mexico finished with four wins from five and runners-up spot in the group.

THE KEY PLAYER

Having shot to fame at France '98, where his white boots and Caniggia-style haircut decorated Mexico's surprising advance to the second round, **Cuauhtémoc Blanco** looks as though he is back to something like his best form. A deep-lying forward with a taste for the spectacular, Blanco got nine goals during qualifying – five of them in Mexico's last three matches.

A belated move from Mexican club football to Real Valladolid of Spain has been a mixed blessing, however. While the European experience has made Blanco a more selfless player, it has also seen him afflicted by a series of niggling injuries.

THE EMERGING TALENT

When coach Javier Aguirre looked at the fixture schedule for 2002, he decided to do a deal with the foreign clubs who had Mexican internationals on their books. Aguirre would use only locally based players for the CONCACAF Gold Cup in January, in return for getting his bigger stars together for a training camp prior to the World Cup. One of the unlikely beneficiaries of the deal might just be **Jair García**, a 23-year-old striker from the Guadalajara club who scored half an hour into his debut to give Mexico a 1–0 Gold Cup win over El Salvador.

THE DUGOUT

After Manuel Lapuente and Enrique Meza had failed, the Mexican FA got third time lucky with **Javier Aguirre** during qualifying. A veteran of the 1986 side (he was sent-off in extra time during Mexico's quarter-final defeat by West Germany), Aguirre brought the squad back to basics, using a simple 4–4–2 formation and giving recalls to some overlooked older players. However, as his innovative approach to the Gold Cup showed, Aguirre is more open to fresh ideas than his critics sometimes give him credit for.

Aguirre's realism revived Mexico's qualifying campaign

BELGIUM

In making this their sixth successive World Cup, the Belgians broke the record for the number of consecutive appearances in the finals by a team that has not qualified automatically as hosts or holders. A trivial point, perhaps, but it does demonstrate how this modest European nation, with a weak domestic league and few stars playing abroad, has made a virtue out of its limited resources.

THE PEDIGREE

Go back six World Cups to the inaugural game of **Spain '82**, and you find Belgium beating the then reigning champions, Argentina, 1–0, in a display of typical resourcefulness. They went on to defeat El Salvador and draw with Hungary, before falling to Poland and the Soviet Union in the second-round group stage.

The backbone of that Belgian side (goalkeeper Jean-Marie Pfaff, diminutive midfield dynamo Wilfried van Moer and striker Jan Ceulemans) had already guided their country to runners-up spot at the 1980 European Championship. At **Mexico '86**, with van Moer replaced by a gifted play-maker called Enzo Scifo, they got within one step of a World Cup final. Recovering from an opening defeat by the hosts, Belgium beat Iraq, the Soviet Union (4–3 in a thriller after extra time) and then Spain on penalties. A Maradona wonder-goal beat them in the semi-finals, and the Belgians had to settle for fourth place – their best World Cup finish yet.

Since then the country's achievements have been less spectacular, but Belgium have usually entertained us along the way. Scifo hit the woodwork from 30 yards before David Platt's last-minute winner for England at **Italia '90**; Philippe Albert snatched a memorable win over their arch-rivals Holland at **USA '94**; and in France four years ago, the Dutch again failed to beat their neighbours, despite Belgium surrendering 75% of the possession (not to mention 85% of the crowd) in Paris.

THE ROAD TO JAPAN/KOREA

Croatia and Scotland were always going to represent Belgium's biggest hurdles in qualifying. Against the Scots, a late comeback from two-down saved a point at Hampden in March 2001, while a 2–0 win in Brussels the following September delivered an all but fatal blow to Craig Brown's side. Against the Croats there was stalemate in Brussels followed by a 1–0 defeat in Zagreb.

By that time, the Belgians were already assured of at least a place in the play-offs – a position from which they had qualified for the World Cup twice before. **Gert Verheyen** got the only goal of the first leg against the Czechs in Brussels, and after soaking up constant pressure from the home side in Prague in the return, **Marc Wilmots** converted a spot-kick to earn that record-breaking sixth consecutive berth.

Belgium have a team spirit many larger nations covet

THE KEY PLAYER With more than 50 caps and four World Cups already to his name, **Marc Wilmots** is Belgian dependability personified. The attack-minded midfielder through whom a lot of the *Diables Rouges'* best moves are channelled, he had not normally been thought of as much of a goalscorer prior to the qualifying phase for Japan/Korea, which saw him score eight.

After spending a season with Bordeaux in 2000/01, Wilmots returned to German club Schalke – where he has played the best of his club football and where his understanding with Belgian striker Emile Mpenza brings a useful benefit to the national side.

THE EMERGING TALENT Scoring goals has rarely come naturally to the Belgians, but if they are still searching for a natural in front of goal as the finals approach, they may just find salvation in **Wesley Sonck**. Commanding in the air and quick on his feet, Sonck has 68 goals to his name after five seasons in the Belgian first division – the last two with ambitious Racing Genk. So far, though, he has played just four times for his country.

THE DUGOUT Belgium's first-round exit from Euro 2000, which they co-hosted with Holland, almost spelled the end of the road for coach **Robert Waseige**. The affable 62-year-old had had less than a year in the job, and the Belgian FA decided to give him the benefit of the doubt. Waseige has repaid their faith by subtly rebuilding the side while keeping its core intact. Away from the pressure of Brussels, his patient tinkering might yet result in another Belgian World Cup fairytale.

JAPAN

The co-hosting of the World Cup sees Japanese football at an awkward stage in its development. The national side has come on in leaps and bounds since its debut in the finals four years ago, yet while some of Japan's hottest talents have earned transfers abroad, they are not yet getting what their coach Philippe Troussier insists is "the next big step forward" – regular first-team football in Europe's toughest leagues. This unlikely footballing nation, which has only really fallen in love with the game over the past decade, will give the team all the support it can come June. The big breakthrough might have to wait another four years.

THE PEDIGREE

After a series of near-misses, several of which involved their arch-rivals South Korea progressing to the finals in their stead, Japan finally qualified for their first World Cup in **France** four years ago. It was a useful and memorable experience, but not a particularly successful one. They lost all three of their games – against Argentina, Croatia and Jamaica – and scored only once, when it was too late.

Cheered on by thousands of European-based Japanese, some of whom paid as much as £500 for their tickets, Takeshi Okada's side defended stoutly – Argentina and Croatia managed only two goals between them. They also played some neat football in midfield, admittedly against teams not known for monopolising possession. But they failed to give their strikers the ammunition the needed.

Troussier guided Japan to silver in the Confederations Cup

THE ROAD TO JAPAN/KOREA

With four years to go before the next World Cup and no qualifying games to play, the Japanese FA gambled on giving an experienced foreign coach free rein on the squad. Frenchman Philippe Troussier began work almost immediately after the '98 finals, and the gamble quickly paid off.

In 2000 Japan won the Asian Cup for only the second time in their history, and a year later they were runners-up to France in the FIFA Confederations Cup – a fairly meaningless event to most of its participants but, being co-hosted by Japan and Korea, a useful World Cup dress rehearsal for the Asians.

Since then the Japanese have notched up some decent results, holding Italy to a goalless draw in Saitama. The significance of such exhibition games, however, is still to be proven.

THE KEY PLAYER

The youngest man ever to be named Asian footballer of the year when he won the accolade in 1998, **Hidetoshi Nakata** has everything – except a consistent club career. The attacking midfielder played a key role in getting Japan to France '98, and was signed by Italian club Perugia before the finals were over. He became an overnight sensation, scoring twice in his opening game, drawing thousands of Japanese fans to Perugia's *Serie A* matches and inspiring a whole industry of licensed products back home.

But Nakata's £13million transfer from Perugia to Roma in January 2000 did not result in the added glory it was intended to bring. 'Hide' played only a bit-part role in Roma's 2000/01 Italian title triumph, and at his own request he was moved on to Parma (this time for more than £18million) at the end of the season. The transfer resulted in more first-team football, but in less happy circumstances, Nakata's occasional glimpses of magic providing light relief in a battle against relegation.

THE EMERGING TALENT

The top Premiership clubs think nothing of spending £4million on a squad player, as **Junichi Inamoto** has discovered. The 20-year-old midfielder's transfer from Gamba Osaka to Arsenal has resulted in only a handful of first-team appearances, yet Arsène Wenger, himself a veteran of Japan's J-League, rates Inamoto as an excellent passer of the ball, with a physical resilience which can only improve with age and maturity.

THE DUGOUT

The first foreigner to be named Asian coach of the year, **Philippe Troussier** won that accolade after guiding Japan to victory in the Asian Cup in 2000. Just as significantly, a year earlier he had taken the country to glory in the World Youth Championship – an experience which gave him a vital insight into the strengths (and weaknesses) of Japan's next generation. The question now is whether he can bring that generation on sufficiently for them to make an impact on this World Cup.

RUSSIA   After their calamitous failure to qualify for either the last World Cup or Euro 2000, the Russians are back on the big stage and seem determined to make the most of their time in the spotlight. With a gifted squad and a coach who, unusually for Russia, has earned the trust of his players, the nation is quietly confident that 2002 will signal a genuine return to form of one of the global game's great powers. On the other hand, as any Russian football fan will tell you, there have been plenty of false dawns before.

THE PEDIGREE   Until 1994, the Russians competed in the World Cup as the Soviet Union. But there was more to the Soviets than Russia. In fact, many of the old USSR's greatest players – men like Oleg Blokhin and Alexandr Chivadze – were not Russian at all, hailing instead from outlying republics such as the Ukraine, Georgia or Belarus.

The national side, the *sbornaya*, was not encouraged to play in international tournaments until after World War II, and did not make its first World Cup appearance until the 1958 finals in **Sweden**. Captained by Igor Netto and with the legendary Lev Yashin in goal, the Soviets reached the quarter-finals – then showed they were no flash in the pan by winning the inaugural European Championship two years later.

Yashin was still in goal when the Soviets travelled to **England** for the **1966** tournament, where they would lose narrowly to West Germany in the semi-finals – still their best World Cup performance to date. For the next two decades the USSR would normally send a capable enough squad to the finals, but a lack of spontaneity, particularly when things against them, tended to limit them to a place in the last eight or so.

An exception to the rule was the was the *sbornaya* of 1986, led by (Ukrainian-born) European footballer of the year Igor Belanov, which unluckily lost 4–3 to Belgium in the quarter-finals after a series of dubious offside decisions had gone against them.

By the time of **USA '94**, the USSR had broken up. FIFA decided Russia was the natural successor state, and a string of non-Russians, including Ukrainian-born Andrei Kanchelskis, stuck with the team that had a chance of playing in major tournaments rather than play for their place of birth. Or at least, they intended to until a dispute over money resulted in six of them quitting the team on the eve of the tournament – consigning another World Cup to the list of Russian disappointments.

THE ROAD TO JAPAN/KOREA A last-minute defeat in Slovenia notwithstanding, Russia's progress to the finals was as smooth as anyone dared hope. With revitalised players such as **Alexander Mostovoi** and **Vladimir Beschastnykh** scoring freely, Switzerland and Yugoslavia were both eliminated with scarcely any more effort than was required to defeat the group's minnows, Luxembourg and the Faroe Isles. The Russians finished three points clear at the top, Beschastnykh providing the perfect finale with a hat-trick in a 4–0 mauling of the Swiss in Moscow.

THE KEY PLAYER At the age of 33, **Alexander Mostovoi** is as influential for his country he has ever been. Nicknamed 'the Tsar' by fans of Celta Vigo, the Spanish club where he has been playmaker for the past six years, Mostovoi squandered his last big chance to shine at international level, providing only a few fancy flicks (and a couple of missed sitters) as Russia crashed out of Euro '96.

Yet under the same coach – Oleg Romantsev – who endured those disappointments six years ago, Mostovoi has blossomed again, his vision if anything keener than it once was, his ability to turn a game still unmatched by any of his compatriots.

THE EMERGING TALENT Captain of Spartak Moscow, twice Russia's footballer of the year, **Yegor Titov** is still relatively unknown outside his homeland. A gifted but unpredictable forward, he is sometimes accused of going AWOL during internationals – in stark contrast to his consistent form for his club. Now 25, Titov may see the World Cup as a useful shop window for his talents; if so, he will have to stand up and be counted.

Titov could have a better scoring record for his country

THE DUGOUT Few coaches manage to combine running a club and a national team at the same time. Fewer still have two goes at it. Yet Spartak Moscow boss **Oleg Romantsev** remains the only man capable of getting inside the minds of Russia's wayward stars and, for as long as he retains that ability, his desire to do two jobs simultaneously will be accommodated by Russia's hard-pressed FA.

TUNISIA North Africa's only representatives at this World Cup, the Tunisians are already showing signs that they may struggle to live with the burden of that status. A normally enterprising team whose attacking talents have been honed among some of Africa's strongest club sides, Tunisia flopped badly at the African Nations Cup earlier this year, failing to progress beyond the group stage after failing to score in their three games – piling the pressure on recently appointed coach Henri Michel.

THE PEDIGREE Regardless of how they do in Japan/Korea, the Tunisians will always have a place in World Cup history as the first African nation to win a match at the finals. Their 3–1 victory over Mexico in **Argentina** in 1978 was no less than their neat, instinctive football deserved, and only bad luck – and the woodwork – prevented further progress from a group that also contained two powerhouses of the game at the time, Poland and West Germany.

Tunisia scratched an 20-year itch to return to the World Cup in **France** four years ago where, despite the promise of a new generation of players, conditions which should have suited them and vociferous support from the French *maghreb* community, they managed only a point from three games – and then when it was too late, against a Romanian side which had already qualified for the second phase.

This year's tournament is a second chance for that same generation, originally grouped together as an Under-23 side to compete at the Atlanta Olympics of 1996, to show the world what they can do. But they will have to overcome their fear of committing men forward to do so.

Vociferous support was to no avail in France four years ago

THE ROAD TO JAPAN/KOREA
Having beaten Mauritania home and away to qualify for the group phase, and with a solid bedrock of players including goalkeeper **Chokri el-Ouaer**, playmaker **Zoubeir Beya** and striker **Adel Sellimi**, Tunisia always looked to have too much class for their opponents in what was one of Africa's weaker World Cup sections.

A hapless Congo-Brazzaville, who'd originally withdrawn from the tournament and only relented after being threatened with fines by FIFA, were thrashed 6–0 in Tunis, with Beya scoring twice. The same player then grabbed another double in Tunisia's final game, a 3–0 win away to Congo-Kinshasa last July, which confirmed them as group winners, five points clear of the Ivory Coast.

THE KEY PLAYER Tunisia's tradition of producing nimble, elusive front players has continued at the feet of **Adel Sellimi**. Now 29, he approaches his second World Cup in fine club form but with a question mark hanging over his commitment to the national side.

Sellimi signed on the dotted line for Club Africain of Tunis at the age of 10. He remained there for 14 years, being tempted away only by the lure of a better class of oppoisition in the French league with Nantes. Like so many imports, though, he struggled to get first-team football and jumped at the chance, in the summer of 1998, to form a three-way partnership with fellow Tunisians Zoubeir Beya and Mehdi ben Slimane at German club SC Freiburg. The cut and thrust of *Bundesliga* football seemed to suit Sellimi, but internationally his star was beginning to wane. He made little impact at France '98, was overshadowed by Ziad Jaziri and Ali Zitouni in qualifying for Japan/Korea, and was suspended for the African Nations Cup after failing to turn up a for a friendly against Spain.

THE EMERGING TALENT After being nominated in African young player of the year awards for 2000 and helping his country reach the 2002 World Cup with a succession of vital goals, **Ali Zitouni** is on the verge of becoming a superstar striker, despite being barely out of his teens. An injury sustained while playing for his Tunisian club ruled Zitouni out of this year's African Nations Cup, but he looks certain to be fit in time for Japan/Korea.

THE DUGOUT Frenchman **Henri Michel** is Tunisia's third coach in 18 months, succeeding an Italian, Francesco Scoglio, and a German, Eckhard Krautzen, who secured the team's World Cup finals place. After coaching Cameroon in 1994 and Morocco in '98, Michel knows all about getting the best from African sides – but he needs his injury list to shorten if his team's morale is to rise in time for the finals.

KOREA: INTRODUCTION

The most successful of all Asian nations at World Cup level, South Korea deserves to co-host the 2002 tournament on past achievements alone. Yet there is more to hosting a tournament like this than footballing prowess, and the Koreans – despite a stuttering economy and political upheaval in their own backyard – have gone about their preparations with typical thoroughness, ambition and endeavour.

Every single Korean World Cup stadium is brand new, the organisers deciding against re-using any of the facilities built for the 1988 Olympics. The majority of the grounds are 'football only' with the spectators sitting close to the pitch, and most are quite modestly proportioned – there will be no echoing super-stadia here.

South Korea itself (the peninsula has been divided since the end of the Korean war, and a plan to let North Korea host some World Cup matches came to nothing) is modestly proportioned, and flights and accommodation are already at a premium. **Direct return flights** to Seoul's new Incheon airport were at least £1,000 for an economy class seat at press time, and prices will rise, not fall, as the big kick-off approaches. For once, the internet may be of relatively limited use; if you're desperate, make your travel agent do some work for you. See whether alternatives are available via Holland, Switzerland or Austria – countries not sending teams to the World Cup. Or whether, at the other end, it might be cheaper to go via Hong Kong, Taiwan or mainland China.

When it comes to accommodation, only South Korea's capital, Seoul, is likely to have spare rooms in high-quality hotels. Across the country, many rooms have been block-booked in advance on behalf of the FIFA Family – a catch-all euphemism for sponsors, partners, present and former officials, and other hangers-on. Others have been snapped up by tour operators offering 'executive' travel packages.

To get around the problem, the Korean government is sponsoring places in an approved network of country inns, while many host communities are also offering **accommodation in family homes**. These options promise lodgings that are both more affordable and more interesting than an executive hotel could ever be, but they *must* be booked in advance. First port of call is the government-sponsored website: www.worldinn.com.

BUSAN

South Korea's second largest city is also a the world's third-largest container port, and it is still growing. Such is the demand for its shipping and storage facilities that a new port area is being built to the west of town. But Busan is not just about industry – the 2km-long stretch of **white-sand beach** at Haeundae to the north comes into its own in summer, while closer to the centre of town, Gwangalli Beach is lined with scores of **seafood restaurants** – most of the dishes are raw *sashimi* style, known as *hoe* in Korean.

Busan's population of 4million have their own airport at **Gimhae**, 18km from the centre of town, handling both international and domestic flights. There are direct flights to and from four Japanese cities: Tokyo, Osaka, Nagoya and Fukuoka. Around 35 flights every day make the 1hr trip from Seoul-Incheon to Gimhae and vice-versa.

From Gimhae airport, bus #201 leaves every 30mins for downtown Busan, the journey taking around 30mins. A more frequent (every 8mins) stopping service, #307, takes about 50mins to reach the centre.

Half-hourly **express trains** take between 4hrs and 5hrs to make the journey from Seoul, while **buses** – which can run as frequently as every 10mins at peak times – will take on average about 30mins longer to do the same trip.

THE ARENA

The **Asiad Main Stadium** was completed last September and seats 56,000 – 2,000 fewer when the front-most rows of seats are removed to make room for a running track. As well as three first-phase World Cup matches, Busan is also due to host the **14th Asian Games** between September and October this year, hence the need for athletics to be accommodated here.

The stadium is in the outlying **Younjegu Geojedong** district, served by metro line #1 from downtown Busan. The nearest metro station is Dongrae, around 20mins from the centre, and from which it's about a 20min hike (or a 5min taxi ride) to the ground. Alternatively, buses #28, #35 and #306 all go

Busan's multi-purpose stadium under construction

directly to the ground from Busan's main train station – allow 50–60mins, depending on the traffic.

DAEGU
With a population of 2.5million, Daegu is South Korea's third-largest city. The spiritual home of the peninsula's Buddhist and Confucian cultures, today it is the centre of the nation's textile industry and fancies itself as something of a **style capital**, with local and international fashion houses being offered incentives to relocate here.

The place to soak up Daegu's **thriving retail culture** is its main shopping street, Dongseongno, where the beautiful people of the surrounding Gyeongsang province consume conspicuously. The street is lined with cafés and restaurants as well as fashion stores, many offering *galbi* – the local delicacy of steamed, marinated beef ribs.

Daegu has its own airport, handling mainly domestic traffic but also offering direct flights to and from the Japanese city of Osaka, via a new **international passenger terminal** opened in May 2001. There are 36 flights a day between Daegu and Seoul (journey time 1hr).

Alternatively, **express trains** run every 15–30mins between Daegu's central station and the capital, taking around 3hrs 30mins.

THE ARENA
Unlike some of Korea's new grounds, the **Daegu Main Stadium** has already hosted international football. The opening ceremony of the FIFA Confederations Cup took place in teeming rain here in May 2001, followed by a match between South Korea and France which the visitors won 5–0.

Three-quarters of the arena's 68,000 seats are covered by a **Teflon-coated roof membrane** which protects spectators from the rain while allowing a certain amount of natural light through. The roof's distinctive curves have been designed to echo the structure of traditional Korean thatched-roof houses.

Daegu got its first metro line in 1997, but the Grand Park area, in which the stadium stands, is not yet served by the network. The nearest overground train station is East Daegu, 10km away. A variety of **local buses** get much closer to the ground: #910 from East Daegu station (every 9mins, journey time 35mins); #349 from Daegu central train station (every 8mins, journey 45mins); and #399 from the city's express bus terminal (every 12mins, journey 35mins).

DAEJEON Situated in the heart of South Korea about 150km south of Seoul, Daejeon is a **hi-tech heaven**, playing host to scores of software and research companies and staging regular technology trade fairs. It is also an administrative centre, home to both regional and national government bodies, and a major transport hub.

Daejeon's restaurants simmer with the smell of *samgyetang*, a health-giving local speciality of chicken stuffed with garlic, ginseng, beans, gingko nuts and rice.

The **nearest airport** is at Cheongju, 30mins away by road, but most travelling supporters are likely to arrive from Seoul. The fastest express trains (*Samaeul*, departures every 30mins) make the journey from the capital to Daejeon's main train station in 1hr 30mins, while the *Mugunghwa* service takes 1hr 45mins. Express buses are more frequent (every 5–10mins) but slower, with a journey time of around 2hrs.

THE ARENA The **Daejeon World Cup Stadium** in the verdant Yuseong district has been designed as an intimate, football-only venue, with seating for just over 40,000, a refreshingly simple, cantilevered design and Korea's first retractable stadium roof. Once the World Cup is over it will become home to the local football club, **Daejeon Citizen**.

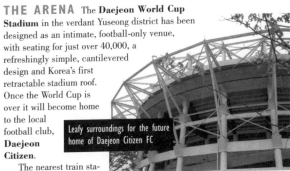

Leafy surroundings for the future home of Daejeon Citizen FC

The nearest train station is West Daejeon, 10km away. Bus #101 runs direct to the ground from here (service every 15mins, journey time 35mins). From Daejeon's **main train station**, buses #104 and #140 (approx every 10mins) take around 50mins, while buses #102 and #103 go from the **express bus terminal** (every 10mins, journey 35mins).

From Seoul-Incheon airport, an 'Airport Limousine' shuttle bus departs hourly direct for the stadium, journey 3hrs 45mins.

GWANGJU

Tucked away in the south-western corner of the Korean peninsula, Gwangju likes to portray itself as a **city of culture** and has scheduled the fourth edition of its *Biennale* arts festival to coincide with the World Cup. It is the birthplace of *pansori*, Korea's unique style of traditional narrative song, and its National Museum houses a priceless collection of art and relics from the Baekje and Joseon dynasties.

But Gwangju also has another tradition – that of **political rebellion**. It was here that the volunteer armies opposed to Japanese invaders in the 16th century organised themselves and where Korea's modern independence movement took shape between 1910 and 1945.

There's little hint of revolution in the air these days, but Gwangju's cultured atmosphere, relaxed pace (by Korean standards) and striking scenery make it an attractive spot. Even the local delicacy, *tteokgalbi* – essentially a grilled, marinated hamburger – seems likely to suit foreign visitors' tastes.

Gwangju's small **domestic airport** has five flights a day from Seoul (journey time 1hr). Eight *Saemaeul* express trains leave Seoul each day (journey around 4hrs) in addition to 18 *Mugunghwa* services taking 30mins longer. Express buses (every 10mins at peak times) also do the journey in about 4hrs.

THE ARENA

The **Gwangju World Cup Stadium** has been built in the Seo-gu district, about 6km from the centre of town. It has a capacity of just under 43,000 and, like the Daejeon stadium, has been built only with football in mind. Spectators sit close to the pitch, about two-thirds of them having the benefit of the arena's gently curving roof.

Local bus #36 (every 12mins, journey time 25mins) leaves for the stadium from Gwangju's **main train station**, calling at the Gwangcheon express bus terminal along the way. You can also get to the ground direct from Gwangju airport using bus #106, but this runs infrequently and takes around 30mins to complete its journey, traffic permitting.

INCHEON

Such is the extent to which Seoul has sprawled that Incheon, 30km away to the west and a city in its own right, can feel like a suburb of the capital. The two are in any case inextricably linked by history and by commerce, Incheon acting as **Seoul's gateway to the sea** and now, thanks to the construction of a brand-new international airport here, its gateway to the world as well.

Incheon owes its current wealth and importance to the decline of the Joseon dynasty and the end of its iso-lationist policy toward trade in the late 19th century. Like Kobe in Japan, Incheon became an interna-tional trading post – with China in particular – and this was reflected in the make-up of its population; there has been a **Chinatown** here since 1883.

A site for sore eyes as the Munhak stadium takes shape

Down by the water-front, restaurants serve up **freshly caught seafood** from the Yellow Sea – look out for *kkotgejjim* (steamed blue crab) and *kkotgetang* (spicy blue crab soup). For a complete change of pace, Jayu Park offers fine views of the port and across the sea to Wolmido island.

Incheon international airport opened in March 2001 and served more than 100 million passengers in its first year.

THE ARENA The **Incheon Munhak Stadium** is in the Nam-gu district and has been built as part of a larger multi-sports complex. It was one of the first of Korea's new stadia to commence building (in July 1994) and one of the last to be completed, in December 2001. Its distinctive oval-shaped roof, which forms part of a 'sail and mast' construction to reflect Incheon's maritime links, provides protection from the elements for all 50,000 spectators.

Incheon has its own **metro system**, run separately from – but linked to – that of neighbouring Seoul. Take Line #1 of the latter as far as Bupyeong and change there onto the Incheon network. Munhak Stadium has its own new metro stop, a 5min walk from the ground. Allow about 1hr for the whole journey from downtown Seoul. From central Incheon, buses #4, #6, #13 and #27 all take around 15mins to get to Munhak.

JEONJU A city rich with the relics of its past as seat of the Joseon dynasty's ruling families, Jeonju is one of the few Korean conurbations which feels as though it is still in touch with its history. Surrounded by pagodas and boasting the best-preserved old town in South Korea, it draws visitors from all over the country with the quality of its historic monuments and a varied programme of traditional festivals.

The stadium's four concave roofs form a symbolic fan shape

Yet Jeonju is not a museum town. The local dish, a multi-flavoured risotto-type affair called *bibimbap*, is shortly to be trademarked so that it can be profitably exported around the world. And when it came to building a new stadium for the World Cup, the Jeonju authorities chose a modern yet elegant design that is arguably the most **architecturally successful** of all Korea's 2002 arenas.

Jeonju has a **domestic airport** at Gunsan, 60km away, but most fans will arrive from Seoul by land. There's little to choose between the Saemaeul trains and express buses as both take around 3hrs to reach downtown Jeonju. There are 16 trains a day, while buses depart every 10mins or so.

THE ARENA Jeonju is famous for its fans and its music, and the **Jeonju World Cup Stadium** has been designed to evoke both. Its four concave roofs have been designed to echo the shape of a traditional Joseon-period fan, while the suspension cables which support them represent the 12 strings of a Gaya harp. The stadium holds only 42,000 but the area it occupies makes it the largest of all Korea's new grounds.

Local buses #225 and #336 leave from the express bus terminal in **downtown Jeonju** every 20mins, taking 30–40mins to reach the ground, depending on traffic. If you're arriving at the train station, take bus #70–5 or #79–1 as far as the World Cup Stadium intersection, and change on to the #225 or #336 there.

SEOGWIPO

The island of Jeju-do occupies a unique place in Korean culture, being to Seoul or Busan what Hawaii is to New York or Chicago. South Korea's **leading tourist destination** was formed by volcanic activity about a million years ago, and Mount Hallasan, Korea's highest peak which dominates the resort of Seogwipo on Jeju-do's south coast, has been shaped by molten rock over the past 250,000 years.

The unique cliff formations and waterfalls which surround Seogwipo are further testament to the island's violent past, but today Jeju-do could scarcely be more placid – **a tropical haven** for honeymooners, families and the occasional foreign dignitary summoned to one of the summit meetings in which Seogwipo specialises.

Seogwipo itself is tiny, being home to fewer than 100,000 people – though its population increases substantially in peak holiday periods. Hotel space is at a premium at any time of year, and the island's capital, Jeju City (about an hour's drive from Seogwipo) has more in the way of accommodation, retail and business facilities – particularly the Yeondong district.

The island's **airport** is at Jeju City. There are between 35 and 45 flights a day between Seoul and Jeju (journey time 1hr 10mins).

THE ARENA

Perhaps the most striking of all Korea's stadium designs, the **Jeju World Cup Stadium** makes the most of its spectacular waterfront location. A curved concrete roof, elevated off the ground by suspension cables, covers half the stadium, providing cover for about 20,000 of the 42,000 seats. The remainder of the seating is open-air, but protected from the elements – and Jeju-do's high winds in particular – by being carefully angled and sunk into the ground. The stands are close to the pitch, which is itself 14m below ground level.

The overall shape has been designed to suggest an *oreum* – a type of **volcanic crater** of which about 300 are dotted around the slopes of Mount Hallasan. Regardless of its inspiration, it is a breathtaking sight.

From Jeju airport, an 'Airport Limousine' **shuttle bus** runs every 15mins during the day, taking just over an hour to reach the stadium. The same service calls at central Seogwipo, 15mins away from the ground, along the way. Alternatively, local buses #6, #11, #100 and #120 run every 10–20mins from the town centre to the stadium, taking 20mins to reach their destination.

SEOUL

From the ashes of the Korean war, Seoul has risen to become one of the world's largest cities, a **vibrant metropolis** of more than 10million souls which sprawls for mile after mile.

Seoul has been **Korea's capital** ever since the Joseon dynasty was established here in 1392, but it also enjoyed a period as the peninsula's political and economic centre well before then, when the region was under the sway of the Baekje dynasty. The legacy of these rulers can be seen in everything from prehistoric fragments in the city's museums to fortresses, palaces and temples. Blink, though, and you'd miss them – those that aren't standing in their own gardens tend to be tucked down alleyways between the city's gleaming skyscrapers.

For **shopping and eating**, the Myeongdong district is currently the place to be. Seoul's best-known regional dish, *gimchi*, is a strange concoction of pickled vegetables, spices and seafood, which is said to offer a health-giving combination of benign bacteria as it ferments. Fortunately, dishes from other Korean regions, not to mention western styles and fast-food joints, are not hard to find in Myeongdong.

Seoul's new **international airport** is out at Incheon (see p.70), leaving the former international hub, Gimpo, to act primarily as a domestic terminal. Gimpo has its own stop on line #5 of Seoul's ever-expanding **metro network** which, at the last count, had 262 stations and nearly 400km of track. (Remarkably, the first line didn't open until 1974.)

THE ARENA

Despite having the legacy of hosting the 1988 Olympics at their disposal, the Seoul authorities were not prepared to have

their city over-shadowed by smaller rivals in the run-up to the World Cup. The result is the **Seoul World Cup Stadium**, which

> The Seoul World Cup Stadium will host the inaugural match

will host the tournament's opening ceremony and inaugural match on 31 May, as well as one other group game and a semi-final. In contrast to the Seoul's Olympic facilities, the stadium has been built for football only. It holds 65,000 people and its light, almost delicate-looking roof provides cover for most of them.

The stadium has had **its own metro station** built for it on metro line #6. From Seoul's main train station, take metro line #4 and change for line #6 at Samgakji.

SUWON

An hour's drive south of Seoul lies a city once designed to replace it as Korea's capital – Suwon. It was in the 18th century that King Jeongjo of the Joseon dynasty founded the city, to which he wanted to move his court so that he could be closer to his father's tomb. The shift in the balance of power lasted only as long as Jeongjo, but some elements of his 18th-century town planning (notably the great fortress of Hwaseong) remain, rubbing shoulders with the office blocks of **hi-tech companies** who made Suwon their base toward the end of the 20th century.

Compared with some of Korea's host cities, Suwon has a fairly compact centre. The dish most commonly found in restaurants here is *Suwon galbi*, a local take on grilled, marinated beef.

The easiest way to get to Suwon is by bus. 'Airport Limousine' services run from both Incheon and Gimpo airports, with departures every 20mins and a journey time of about 90mins.

THE ARENA

A joint venture between Korea's Samwoo Construction Company and the French contractors responsible for the Stade de France, the **Suwon World Cup Stadium** was completed in May last year. Its unique wing-shaped roof is meant to express the potential of the future, while the materials used are intended to harmonise with the historic buildings of the Suwon area.

The arena has an all-seated capacity of 43,000, and is part of a larger sports complex that includes an indoor swimming people and a golf range. Other facilities planned here include conferencing facilities.

From Suwon's main train station, local buses #2, #720 and #13–2 all make the journey out to Paldal-gu, where the ground is situated. Allow about 20mins.

ULSAN

Korean football has its roots in the factory teams of industrial conglomerates, so it is only natural that Ulsan, the **industrial powerhouse** of the nation, should be considered the unofficial capital of the local game. This is the base from which household names such as Hyundai Motors, LG and Samsung launched their global empires, and to this day the biggest local club bears the name Ulsan Hyundai Tigers.

About 40% of Ulsan's 1million population are in their 20s or 30s, giving the city a **dynamic, uptempo feel** and plenty of nightlife options away from the sprawling 'Ulsan Industrial Complex'.

Ulsan has its own **domestic airport**, receiving about 17 flights a day from Seoul Gimpo (journey time 1hr). *Saemaeul* trains (14 daily) take 5hrs, while *Mugunghwa* services are slightly quicker. Express buses leave every 15mins at peak times and also take around 5hrs.

Multi-lingual signs point the way around the Munsu

THE ARENA

As well as the sea to the east, which provides Ulsan with the means to host world-beating shipbuilding among other industries, the region has another point of reference – the mountains which range down its western side. One of these is Mount Munsu, which has given its name to the **Munsu Football Stadium**.

As might be expected from a football hotbed, there is no provision for a running track here, and the bulk of the 43,000 spectators will sit close to the pitch. Typically, the ground's builders approached its construction as if it were a production line, assembling pre-formed parts on-site to reduce the time taken for completion to just three-and-a-half years.

From Ulsan airport, **local buses** #20, #24, #120 and #124 run directly to the ground, with service intervals between 12 and 20mins – journey time 50mins. From the main train station, buses #102, #112 and #126 (every 10–15mins) do the journey in 20–25mins. Bus #102 originates at the express bus terminal, 5mins earlier.

JAPAN: INTRODUCTION

Korea may have the footballing heritage and the sporting infra-structure, but Japan has the professionalism, the passion and the political power. Having come late to the soccer party, the Japanese are making up for lost time with an apparently insatiable appetite for football merchandising, television, websites and the rest.

The hope is that this enthusiasm will prove infectious, and make Japan an entertaining place in which to watch the World Cup. It already promises to be slightly less demanding than South Korea to the western traveller (albeit still, culturally, a radical departure). There are more signs in English, local people are more used to having tourists around, and the transport infrastructure is better-established – Korean Railways can't match the **JR Shinkansen** 'bullet train' for speed.

But Japan will also be more expensive than its neighbour. Its economy may be in a state of sustained 'stagflation', but this is still a very affluent country – as the £6 you will be charged for a bottle of *Kirin* lager shows.

For flights and accommodation, the same advice applies as for Korea (see p.66). Many of the flight tickets – and most of the executive hotel rooms – are already gone, and those who wait risk having to pay more in the long run. Like the Koreans, though, the Japanese have launched a programme of country-inn and **'home stay'** accommodation. Advance booking is essential, so give the website a try: www.itcj.or.jp.

Although supporters are being discouraged from travelling to either country **without match tickets**, it is unclear what level of touting will be tolerated outside stadia, or what sort of prices 'unofficial' tickets will command. With all applications for tickets through official channels now closed, however, anyone considering travelling to the other side of the world without any means of getting into a game when they get there should weigh up the risks carefully.

IBARAKI

IBARAKI An hour north-east of Tokyo, Ibaraki is not a city but a 'prefecture' – a provincial region embracing several towns which successfully bid to host World Cup games in 2002. When you consider that one of Ibaraki's cities is Kashima, one of the Japanese **J-League's best-established bases**, you begin to understand why matches are being hosted here, and not in nearby Tokyo.

Adjacent to Kashima is Mito, Ibaraki's **prefectural capital**. It has a few more sights and a little more history than its neighbour, having been one of the centres of Japanese political authority during the Tokugawa Era (between the 17th and mid-19th centuries) when it was a home to a number of notable scholars and religious leaders. But neither town has much to commend it as a World Cup base, and Tokyo seems a better bet than either.

FIFA and J-League food packs are available outside the ground

Kashima-jingu JR (Japan Railway) station is 1hr 30mins from Tokyo and only 1hr from **Narita international airport** by the fastest express train.

THE ARENA One of the few stadia to have been refurbished, rather than built from scratch, for the World Cup finals, the Kashima Soccer Stadium was Japan's first purpose-built football arena when it was opened in 1993. Home to the Kashima Antlers J-League club, after renovations were completed in May 2001 it now boasts an all-seated capacity of 41,000, improved facilities for VIPs and the disabled, better sight-lines and more comfortable seating.

The stadium is 3km from the centre of Kashima and has **its own train station** on the Kashima Rinkai Tetsudo railway line – change at Kashima-jingu if coming from Tokyo, and allow 2hrs for the complete trip. It's a 2min walk from the station to the ground, slightly more if you stop to buy a pre-packaged container of **half-time food** from one the officially licensed stalls.

KOBE

While many of this World Cup's host cities will seem alien to travelling westerners, Kobe is one place where they may just feel at home. This **lively, welcoming port**, sandwiched spectacularly between mountains and sea, was one of industrial Japan's first gateways to the outside world. As an important trading post in the late 19th and early 20th centuries, it introduced the country to a host of outside influences – football among them.

Today the architectural legacy of that era gives the city a surprisingly European feel in places, while a **large expat community** continues to play a significant role in Kobe's commercial, artistic and social life.

Many of the striking new buildings which dot the Kobe skyline have literally risen from the ashes. The devastating **Hanshin-Awaji earthquake** of 1995, which measured 7.3 on the Richter scale, left more than 4,500 Kobe residents dead and a quarter of a million homeless. Many buildings which did not immediately collapse were burned out by one of the estimated 175 fires which broke out in the aftermath of the 'quake.

The nearest airports are Itami for domestic flights and Kansai for international ones. From Itami it's a 40min shuttle-bus ride to the main JR station of Sannomiya. From Kansai, you can take a 1hr 20min JR train ride to Sannomiya, or get the K-JET jetfoil across the bay, which takes just 25mins – shuttle buses connect you to and from the port at either end.

THE ARENA

Local J-League club Vissel Kobe had a perfectly decent home in the Universiade Stadium, built as part of Kobe's preparations for the Student Games of 1985. But that hasn't stopped the construction of a brand-new arena, the **Kobe Wing Stadium**, which will host three World Cup games before being handed over to Vissel as their new home after the tournament is over.

The new stadium has a capacity of 42,000 and was completed last October. It derives its name from its distinctive wing-shaped roof, designed to symbolise **Kobe's rebirth** after the '95 earthquake, though the arena's official name is Misaki Park.

A new branch of the Kagan municipal railway has been built specially to serve the stadium, which has its own station, **Misaki-koen**. The line runs from Sannomiya Hanadokeimae, itself a 5min walk from the JR Sannomiya station which is right next-door; allow 10mins from here to Misaki-koen, then a further 10min walk to the ground.

MIYAGI

The Miyagi prefecture surrounds the **city of Sendai**, some 300km north-east of Tokyo. The region boasts a second-division J-League club, Vegalta Sendai, but not the obsession with football that characterises, say, Kashima or Urawa.

For the Japanese, though, this is a region steeped in political and economic history. It was from Miyagi that Masamune Date, lord of Sendai, sent envoys to establish trade relations with the outside world in 1613. The group visited several European cities, including the Vatican, where they presented a formal letter to Pope Paul V.

Although official Japanese World Cup documentation lists this venue as Miyagi, many FIFA resources refer to it as Sendai. Even more confusingly, the stadium itself is in **Rifu**, a dormitory town about 10km out of downtown Sendai.

Miyagi's 'Samurai helmet' stadium is bold and distinctive

Rifu itself has very little accommodation, but Sendai has more options and is sufficiently 'different' from the Tokyo area to merit a stay, if you have time for one. The strange leaf-shaped things being sold in restaurants and takeaways are *Sasa-kamaboko*, the local speciality of moulded fish paste, which is actually more appetising than it sounds.

Sendai is on a major **JR Shinkansen line**, just under 2hrs from Tokyo. The city also has its own airport; as well as domestic connections there are direct flights from Seoul-Incheon in Korea (flight time 2hrs 40mins).

THE ARENA

Like Korea's Seogwipo design, the **Miyagi Stadium** has a curved roof over half of its length, giving it a novel appearance – though the setting here is less spectacular. The roof has been proportioned so that it is reminiscent of the samurai helmets worn by Masamune Date and other warlords of his era.

The arena holds seats almost 50,000 and is part of the larger Miyagi Prefecture General Athletic Park, which contains a number of other sports facilities.

From **Sendai's JR station** it's a 15min ride on the local JR line to Rifu station. The stadium is a further 15min walk from here, although **shuttle buses** should be in operation on World Cup matchdays.

NIIGATA

Centre of the country's main rice-producing region and the only Japanese World Cup venue to be situated on the west (Sea of Japan) coast of Honshu island, Niigata once traded as much with China, Korea and Russia as with Tokyo. But JR's Joetsu Shinkansen line now connects this once isolated area directly with the capital, tunnelling under the mountain ranges which run down the centre of Honshu and reducing the journey time between Tokyo and Niigata to a paltry 1hr 40mins.

Like Sendai, however, Niigata is an attractive destination in its own right and deserves to be stayed in, rather than commuted to from the capital. Climatically it is **noticeably less humid** in summer here than on Japan's Pacific coast, and since rice is central to everything, it seems only natural that Niigata *sake* is reckoned to be the best in Japan.

As well as the Joetsu Shinkansen, two other JR 'bullet train' services converge on Niigata. The city also has its own **international airport**, with direct flights to/from Osaka-Itami, Nagoya and Sapporo in Japan, as well as Seoul-Incheon in Korea.

THE ARENA

Another laudably distinctive design, the **Niigata 'Big Swan' Stadium** derives its nickname both from the shape of its roof and from the swans which traditionally inhabit the adjacent natural lake.

That swan-shaped roof covers 90% of the new arena's 42,000 seats, and the stadium's designers are setting particular store by the ground's internal accessibility – wheelchair ramps are everywhere, there are special areas of 'family' seating, and the whole place is barrier-free.

The stadium is on the outskirts of Niigata and has no train station of its own. However, **frequent shuttle buses** will link the ground with the city's main JR station – journey time is expected to be 15–20mins, depending on traffic. Regular shuttles will also connect the JR station with Niigata's airport, journey time around 30mins.

OITA

The southernmost of Japan's four main islands, **Kyushu** is a region of hot springs and tropical storms. Historically quite isolated from Honshu to the north, it is endeavouring to become better integrated into the Japanese mainstream while retaining its own cultural identity. Kyushu's major port, Oita, promises to be a fascinating World Cup venue.

While spa resorts and thermal baths are the region's historical tourist attractions, football is gaining in popularity among the local populace, and Oita is in the process of trying to attract a J-League team to the area. The construction of the city's so-called 'Big Eye' stadium is the latest stage in this process.

Although it is possible to catch a jetfoil (journey time 3hrs) or car ferry (14hrs) from **Busan in Korea** to the Kyushu port of Hakata-ko, most fans are likely to arrive by plane at Oita's international airport, which gets direct flights from Tokyo-Haneda, Osaka-Kansai and Seoul-Incheon.

THE ARENA

Designed to blend in with the hills that surround it, the **Oita 'Big Eye' Stadium** gets its nickname from its roof, which is said to resemble an eye when open. The roof is all-encompassing and fully retractable – one of the largest of its kind anywhere in the world. A translucent material has been used so that sunlight continues to filter through to the pitch when the roof is closed. The stadium holds 43,000 and was completed in May last year. A unique 'Sky Camera' situated in the middle of the roof, provides an overhead view of the pitch which is then beamed onto a giant screen inside the arena.

From Oita airport, it's a 30min hovercraft ride across the bay to **Oita City's Nishi-Shimchi port**, from where shuttle buses depart for the main JR train station (journey 15mins). To save changing,

Oita's 'Big Eye' closes its lid for the cameras

you can take a bus all the way from the airport to the station, but this takes slightly longer and is a less scenic way to go. From the station, it's a 15min **shuttle-bus ride** to the stadium, which is about 7km out of town.

OSAKA

A sprawling metropolis with strong social and economic ties to neighbouring Kobe and Kyoto, **Osaka means business**. The opening of the new international airport of Kansai has turned it into a major transport hub, and many Japanese corporations have their headquarters here.

Osaka is not, on the face of it, the most attractive World Cup host city. But its transport links make it a very practical base, while its reputation as Japan's **gastronomic capital** and its colourful nightlife are two further fine reasons to stay.

While Kansai handles most international and some domestic services, the Osaka region's original airport, Itami, to the north of town, still handles some routes. From Tokyo-Haneda you can fly to either, from Tokyo-Narita only to Itami. None of these options takes more than about 1hr 15min, but a more scenic option (and one that gets you straight into the centre of Osaka) is to use the JR Shinkansen a 3hr ride from Tokyo to Shin-Osaka station.

Coming from Korea, both Busan and Seoul-Incheon have direct flights to Kansai (flight times 1hr 30min and 2hrs respectively).

THE ARENA

Though built as recently as 1996, Osaka's **Nagai Stadium** has an almost quaint air about it by comparison with some of the World Cup's newer, bolder venues.

A nine-lane running track separates the ground's 50,000 seats from the pitch, and only two-thirds of spectators are under cover from the elements. On the credit side, a complete lack of supporting pillars means all fans have an unobstructed view of the action.

Nagai is about 10km from downtown Osaka and, somewhat confusingly, has two different train stations. One is on JR's local **Hanwa Line**, a 10–15min walk from the ground. The other is on the **Midosuji Line** of Osaka's efficient city metro system – it's closer to the ground but, depending on where you're staying in Osaka, the train ride itself will almost certainly take longer. Either way, allow at least 45mins for the complete journey from downtown Osaka.

SAITAMA

SAITAMA To many outsiders, the absence of 'Tokyo' from the list of Japan's World Cup host cities came as a shock. But while it is true that the capital itself will not host any games, the prefecture of Saitama is so close that it is effectively part of **Tokyo's metropolitan area**. And while Tokyo itself is not known for its love of football, Saitama couldn't be more different – local J-League team **Urawa Red Diamonds** are one of the best-supported in the country, while neighbouring Omiya City boasts second-division club Omiya Ardija.

The city of Urawa itself has a youthful, dynamic air in keeping with its recent huge economic growth and prosperity. On the other hand, transport links to central Tokyo are so good – and accommodation in Saitama so relatively scarce – that 'commuting' to and from the capital is probably not a bad idea.

The region's main JR train station is Saitama Shin-Toshin, but the **'Saitama New Metropolitan Center'** in which the stadium has been built also has its own station, **Urawa-Misono**, served by both the Saitama Kosoku Tetsudo Railway (a 50min ride from JR Tokyo, change at Oji) and the Nanboku Line of Tokyo's subway system.

There is also a direct bus service (journey time 2hrs) from **Narita airport**, Tokyo's main international gateway, to Saitama Shin-Toshin station, from where it's a 5min train ride to Higashi-Kawaguchi and a further 5min to Urawa-Misono by either overground or subway routes. Fans arriving at Tokyo's main hub for domestic services, **Haneda airport**, should take the monorail shuttle to Hamamatsucho JR station, then a 5min train ride to JR Tokyo and travel via Oji from there (see above).

THE ARENA Less than 10km from the centre of Urawa city, the **Saitama Stadium** is a proud testament to the region's passion for football. Its capacity of 63,700 makes it the biggest Japanese stadium dedicated to football, and one of the largest in Asia. The majority of spectators are under cover, but there is no sense that the ground's atmosphere or the playability of its pitch have been compromised to satisfy an architect's whim. The main stand is only 14m from the pitch, and a total of 27 gates should make this one of the World Cup's most hassle-free venues to enter and leave.

How you approach the stadium will depend on where you're staying in Tokyo. If you're north of the centre and don't want the hassle of travelling into town, then use the metro's Nanboku Line (allow 1hr 15min). Anywhere else, and it makes sense to head for JR Tokyo and use the Saitama Kosoku Tetsudo line

World Cup posters line the streets of soccer-mad Urawa

from Oji instead. Urawa-Misono station is about a 15min walk from the ground.

SAPPORO
No other venue provides more of a contrast with Japan's other cities than Sapporo, capital of the northern island of **Hokkaido**. With its lush vegetation, temperate climate and (unusually for Japan) proliferation of meadows and dairy farms, Hokkaido will feel more like northern Europe than any other 2002 World Cup region.

Yet Sapporo is still emphatically a Japanese city, its booming economy having helped it to its current position as the fifth largest in the land, despite being founded only just over a century ago. If history is thin on the ground here, then sports and leisure facilities are anything but. Winter sports are a major attraction and Sapporo was a memorably successful host of the **Winter Olympics** in 1972. Downtown, meanwhile, the **Susukino district** boasts more than 5,000 shops, restaurants and bars, many of the latter serving up corn-on-the-cob – Sapporo's seemingly ubiquitous snack.

Crowning all this is the Sapporo Dome, home to "the world's first hovering soccer stage" and, even by the high standards of this World Cup, a remarkable triumph of courageous architecture and new technology.

Sapporo's **Shin-Chitose Airport** makes Hokkaido a more accessible prospect than you might imagine. There are more than 300 flights per week between here and Tokyo-Haneda (flight time 1hr 30min), making it the single busiest airline route anywhere in the world. Other domestic

Japanese services connect the airport with Osaka (14 flights daily, divided between Kansai and Itami, journey 2hrs); Sendai (eight daily, journey 1hr 10min); and Niigata (three daily, journey 1hr 15min).

A lookout post atop Sapporo's permanent Dome

There are also five direct flights per week to/from Seoul-Incheon in Korea (2hrs 40min).

THE ARENA The unique **Sapporo Dome** is actually two areas in one. The 'indoor arena', where World Cup matches will be held, is covered by a dome measuring 53,000 square metres – the biggest of its kind in Japan. This effectively shields spectators from the vagaries of Hokkaido's climate but, mindful of the way covered stadia tend to suffer from boggy pitches because the grass is not exposed to sufficient sunlight, the Dome's designers have created an 'outdoor arena' into which the **entire playing surface can be moved**. A glass partition opens electronically along one side of the Dome, and through this the pitch is slowly moved (at a speed of four metres per minute) by 34 wheels, while being kept hovering 7.5cm above the ground by air pressure.

The removable pitch is, in fact, not just there to keep the turf playable. Underneath it in the Dome lies an artificial surface which, thanks to mechanically retractable, rotatable and reconfigurable seating, can be **used for baseball** when the football pitch is moved outside.

For the 54,000 spectators who can use the Dome's indoor arena when it is in 'football' mode, the stadium promises an unforgettable atmosphere (thanks to the acoustics imparted by the 'ceiling') and unsurpassable sight-lines.

The Dome has its own station, **Fukuzumi**, on the Toho line of Sapporo's metro system, a 10min ride from the city's main JR train station. JR trains link the main station with Shin-Chitose Airport (four trains per hour, journey time 40min), but the authorities are also promising to lay on **shuttle buses to run directly** between the airport and Fukuzumi, with an estimated journey time of 45min. Fukuzumi station is about a 10min walk from the Dome.

SHIZUOKA

The beating heart of Japan's football culture and the centre of a tourist region *par excellence*, the prefecture of Shizuoka makes for a **tempting World Cup base**, even though its position midway between Tokyo and Osaka makes it easily accessible from either, and accommodation may not be in plentiful supply. Dominated scenically by Mount Fuji, this as an area of outstanding natural beauty, relatively little impacted by modern industry and with few major conurbations.

It sounds like an unpromising background for football and, in truth, the reasons for Shizuoka's love affair with the game are not easy to pinpoint. But the prefecture was one of the first in Japan to set up its own regional football association, and an ever-growing infrastructure dedicated to the game now includes one of the longest-established training centres in the country, around 1,200 qualified coaches and more than 40,000 registered players. The region has two top-flight J-League teams, **Shimizu S-Pulse** and **Jubilo Iwata**. The latter are the current champions of Asia and will compete in the next FIFA World Club Championship in 2003.

Shizuoka's brand-new World Cup venue is in the **Aino district** of Fukuroi City, more than 50km from Shizuoka City itself. There is no major airport to hand, but Kakegawa station on the **JR Shinkansen** line between Tokyo and Osaka (allow 1hr 30min from Tokyo, 2hrs from Osaka) is only 5min away by regional train.

THE ARENA

The ground is officially known as the **Shizuoka Stadium ECOPA** – the 'ECOPA' bit standing for ECOlogy and PArk. With so much natural beauty (including two national parks) in the surrounding area, the stadium's designers were under enormous pressure to keep the environmental impact of their creation to a minimum, and the whole facility has been designed to make efficient use of resources such as water, heat and light, recycling wherever possible.

The stadium has a running track, but this can be covered by temporary seating during soccer games, resulting in the capacity rising by more than

5,000 to a little over 51,000. The stadium was completed in March 2001, around the same time as **Aino station**, connected to the JR Shinkansen at Kakegawa and about a 10min walk from the ground.

YOKOHAMA

A city with its own distinct historical and commercial identity, even though it adjoins Tokyo and acts as the capital's main sea port, Yokohama will become the focus of attention for billions of people when it hosts **the World Cup final** on 30 June. Japan's second-largest city, it has a population of more than 3.5million and, in contrast to its bigger, more famous neighbour, it also boasts a strong football culture. The city has its own J-League team, the **Yokohama F Marinos**, and it is their home ground, the Yokohama International Stadium, which will host the final along with three first-round fixtures.

Yokohama has no airport of its own and has no need of one – for international flights, **Tokyo's Narita** is only 1hr 30min away by JR Narita Express, while domestic travellers have an even easier run, just 20min on the Keikyu Line from **Haneda airport**.

THE ARENA

The biggest sports arena in Japan, the **Yokohama International Stadium** seats 72,000 and, though completed as recently as October 1997, it has been totally refurbished for the World Cup. The presence of a running track means it is not an ideal soccer venue but, as anyone who has been to a Yokohama F Marinos game will testify, the local fans don't let that stop them creating an atmosphere.

The ground is 6km from downtown Yokohama City, about a 20min walk from **JR Shin-Yokohama station**. This is served by Shinkansen trains from Osaka, but services from Narita, Haneda and other Tokyo stations arrive at the main JR Yokohama terminus, a 10min ride away by metro. If you want to get even nearer to the ground, you can halve the walk by hopping on a regional JR train at Shin-Yokohama and travelling one stop to **Kozukue**.